ARISTOTLE'S *POLITICS*

Continuum *Reader's Guides*

Continuum's *Reader's Guides* are clear, concise and accessible introductions to classic works of philosophy. Each book explores the major themes, historical and philosophical context and key passages of a major philosophical text, guiding the reader towards a thorough understanding of often demanding material. Ideal for undergraduate students, the guides provide an essential resource for anyone who needs to get to grips with a philosophical text.

Reader's Guides available from Continuum:

Aristotle's Nicomachean Ethics – Christopher Warne
Berkeley's Principles of Human Knowledge – Alasdair Richmond
Berkeley's Three Dialogues – Aaron Garrett
Deleuze and Guattari's Capitalism and Schizophrenia – Ian Buchanan
Deleuze's Difference and Repetition – Joe Hughes
Derrida's Writing and Difference – Sarah Wood
Descartes' Meditations – Richard Francks
Hegel's Philosophy of Right – David Rose
Heidegger's Being and Time – William Blattner
Heidegger's Later Writings – Lee Braver
Hobbes's Leviathan – Laurie M. Johnson Bagby
Hume's Dialogues Concerning Natural Religion – Andrew Pyle
Hume's Enquiry Concerning Human Understanding – Alan Bailey
    and Dan O'Brien
Kant's Critique of Pure Reason – James Luchte
Kant's Groundwork for the Metaphysics of Morals – Paul Guyer
Kuhn's The Structure of Scientific Revolutions – John Preston
Locke's Essay Concerning Human Understanding – William Uzgalis
Locke's Second Treatise of Government – Paul Kelly
Mill's On Liberty – Geoffrey Scarre
Mill's Utilitarianism – Henry West
Nietzsche's On the Genealogy of Morals – Daniel Conway
Plato's Republic – Luke Purshouse
Rousseau's The Social Contract – Christopher Wraight
Sartre's Being and Nothingness – Sebastian Gardner
Spinoza's Ethics – Thomas J. Cook
Wittgenstein's Tractatus Logico Philosophicus – Roger M. White

ARISTOTLE'S *POLITICS*

A Reader's Guide

JUDITH A. SWANSON
AND
C. DAVID CORBIN

continuum

Continuum International Publishing Group

The Tower Building   80 Maiden Lane
11 York Road   Suite 704
London SE1 7NX   New York NY 10038

www.continuumbooks.com

British Library Cataloguing-in-Publication Data
A catalogue record for this book is available from the British Library.

ISBN-10: HB: 0-8264-8498-0
          PB: 0-8264-8499-9
ISBN-13: HB: 978-0-8264-8498-7
          PB: 978-0-8264-8499-4

Library of Congress Cataloging-in-Publication Data
Swanson, Judith A. (Judith Ann), 1957–
Aristotle's *Politics*: A Reader's Guide/Judith A. Swanson and
C. David Corbin.
p. cm.
Includes bibliographical references and index.
ISBN 978-0-8264-8498-7 – ISBN 978-0-8264-8499-4
1. Aristotle. Politics. 2. Political science.
I. Corbin, C. David II. Title. III. Title: Politics.

JC71.A7S88 2009
320.01'1–dc22   2008038906

Typeset by Newgen Imaging Systems Pvt Ltd, Chennai, India
Printed and bound in Great Britain by CPI Antony Rowe,
Chippenham, Wiltshire

CONTENTS

Preface   vii
Acknowledgements   viii

1 Context   1
2 Overview of Themes   9
3 Reading the Text   15
  Politics I   15
  Politics II   35
  Politics III   47
  Politics IV   66
  Politics V   82
  Politics VI   99
  Politics VII   107
  Politics VIII   121
4 Reception and Influence   128
5 Guide to Further Reading   149

Notes   155
Index   161

PREFACE

The commentary on the *Politics* provided herein relies on Carnes Lord's translation, and therefore the authors recommend it as a companion to this *Reader's Guide*. Other translations that inform the commentary or that are worth consulting are listed in the back under 'Guide to Further Reading'.

The authors divided the labour as indicated below, with the exception that Judith Swanson wrote the study questions for Books I–VIII and suggested answers to them and arguments to guide the commentaries on Books IV–VII that were written by David Corbin:

Chapter 1: Context – Swanson
Chapter 2: Overview of Themes – Swanson
Chapter 3: Reading the Text

   Commentary on Book I – Swanson
   Commentary on Book II – Swanson
   Commentary on Book III – Swanson
   Commentary on Book IV – Corbin
   Commentary on Book V – Corbin
   Commentary on Book VI – Corbin
   Commentary on Book VII – Corbin
   Commentary on Book VIII – Swanson

Chapter 4: Reception and Influence – Swanson

Judith A. Swanson
C. David Corbin
August 2008

ACKNOWLEDGEMENTS

I would like to thank Continuum Books for inviting me to write this book and David Corbin for accepting my invitation, at a later stage, to join me in the effort.

Judith A. Swanson

I am indebted to Judy Swanson for the opportunity to work on this project. I thank her for teaching me about political philosophy and Aristotle in general and for providing me with an excellent map through which to arrange, engage and explore Books IV–VII of Aristotle's *Politics*.

I thank Esther Moon, undergraduate student at The King's College, and Matthew Parks, Instructor of Political Science at the University of New Hampshire, for their review of my commentary on Books IV and V.

I alone am responsible for all interpretations and errors for the commentary on Books IV–VII.

C. David Corbin

To my father,
Don R. Swanson

CHAPTER 1

CONTEXT

Historical circumstances and an intellectual legacy characterize the context in which Aristotle wrote. This chapter suggests Aristotle's responses to both by portraying him more as a critic than as a partisan. His critical analysis of things political and intellectual emanates from a perspective that sees a necessary and objective linkage between politics and ethics. Political science is not value-neutral and descriptive, but oriented towards the good and thus prescriptive; the human tool of analysis or of science, namely reason, necessarily seeks the good for man, which includes justice. The capacity of reason, an attribute natural to man, to apprehend what is just indicates a natural, objective basis of justice. This chapter discusses Aristotle's concept of natural justice and suggests that it contributes to the unity of Aristotle's corpus.

I BIOGRAPHICAL AND INTELLECTUAL BACKGROUND

Aristotle was born in the year 384 BC in north-eastern Greece in Stagira, a coastal city located on the eastern Chalcidice peninsula, then part of Macedonia. Educated by the philosopher Plato at the Athens Academy, Aristotle himself became a teacher and writer. While in his thirties, he taught throughout the islands of Greece and, at the age of 41, at the request of King Philip II, became tutor to Philip's 13-year-old son, the future King of Macedonia Alexander the Great. (Likewise Philip's father, King Amyntas, had enlisted Aristotle's father, a physician by the name of Nicomachus, into his court.) In 335 BC, when Aristotle was 49 years old, he returned to Athens and founded his own school, the Lyceum. Because of his habit of walking with his students while teaching, his pedagogy became known as 'Peripatetic'. Some of Aristotle's written works appear to be lecture notes, but the total volume, scope and depth of his output indicate as much dedication to posterity as to his living students. Reputed to be handsome and bearded, Aristotle had married a woman named Pythias and, after she died 3 years later, he companioned another woman named Herpyllis. He died at the age of 62, in 322 BC.

Recognition of the character of Aristotle's *Politics* gives us perspective on its historical and intellectual context. The reader recognizes from the start that the text does not mainly report or observe the politics of Athens or of Greek city-states, but rather analyses the origins and characteristic features of polities and politics. Moreover, the analytical approach itself derives from one of the *Politics'* claims about the motivation for political organization or about the origin of politics, namely the desire to live well. In order to satisfy our desire to live well or happily, we must determine what it means to do so, and the possibility of doing so in and out of political society. Aristotle learned to contemplate the meaning and means of living well or of human goodness from his teacher Plato, and it compels him to transcend and criticize his historical context. Responding to his education or intellectual context then, the *Politics* presents, not ancient history but political philosophy.

Likewise, to allege that Aristotle identifies entirely with his peers, namely adult Greek males, simply prejudges him as a conformist – backward, reactionary and incapable of independent thought. Indeed, the sixteenth-century sceptic Montaigne called Aristotle 'the prince of dogmatists', evidently in reference to Aristotle's claims about the political functions of different sorts of individuals, dogmatism supposedly reflective of the culture in which he lived. Yet Montaigne conceded that 'we learn from [Aristotle] that knowing much gives occasion for doubting more'.[1] If, then, as Montaigne suggests, Aristotle complicates or undermines that dogmatism, he does not merely express the prevailing views of his culture. On the contrary, Aristotle's philosophic perspective, acquired from Plato and oriented toward or concerned about the human good, induces him to be critical of the opinions and practices of his contemporaries. Albeit he by no means denounces every one of those opinions and practices, he assesses them throughout the *Politics*.

Aristotle differentiates himself from Plato by adopting an empirical, inductive method that compels him to observe his peers carefully and take seriously their forceful opinions. Inquiry into every matter starts with consideration of what is evident or the case. But while to settle a matter may involve concessions to the status quo, it also incorporates to the extent possible the best scenario.

Furthermore, Aristotle's intellectual context consists of more than Plato per se. Both Plato (interpreting Socrates) and Aristotle respond to not only their contemporaries but to their cultural and intellectual forbearers as well – in particular to poets such as Homer, Aeschylus and Sophocles and to pre-Socratic philosophers such as Heraclitus, Pythagoras and Parmenides. Plato's and Aristotle's direct and indirect responses expanded and introduced two monumental developments in the history of Western civilization: on the one hand, they expanded the concepts of objectivity and knowledge from the divine to the human mind, and on the other they introduced the concept of *political* philosophy.

Prior to pre-Socratic natural philosophers in the West, popular opinion attributed the goings-on of both the physical universe and human relations to the Olympic Gods – arbitrary, unpredictable and capricious sources, a view captured and fostered by poets. By contrast pre-Socratic philosophers sought objective accounts of the cosmos, attributing its composition and movement to particular elements such as fire and water, to mathematical constellations, divine logos, or to one pure Being, for example.[2] After the pre-Socratics, Plato and Aristotle expanded the concept of objective knowledge to account for its comprehension by us; focusing on speech they introduced to Western civilization the concepts of reason, intellect or mind.[3]

Additionally, by arguing that political arrangements and practices reveal truths about human relations, Socrates, Plato and Aristotle introduced to Western civilization objective *political science* – that is, *political philosophy*.[4] Seeking to give a coherent account of political life, political philosophy incorporates objectivity and perceptions of good and bad and just and unjust. Recognizing perceptions or opinions, political philosophy captures and responds to the dynamism inherent in politics while keeping in view government by reason, the best model for the best life.[5] Its ultimate goal is thus practical, namely realization of the best way to live in a given situation.

II ARISTOTLE'S CONCEPT OF NATURAL JUSTICE[6]

Apprehension of the best way to live in a given situation requires apprehension of political justice which, according to Aristotle, is part natural and part legal. Accordingly his ethico-political treatises presuppose and defend the concept of natural right or justice.[7]

Many people do not believe that nature contains or intimates moral guidelines because they infer from physical laws that nature always operates uniformly and they see that human laws, institutions and practices differ from community to community. Nations do not establish the same penalties for murder, but all over the world fire burns wood, rivers flow to oceans and objects fall downward. Noting the uniformity and regularity of physical laws, many people cannot imagine how political justice, which has always varied, can have any natural basis.

It is true, Aristotle affirms, that part of political justice is merely conventional, and thus arbitrary prior to its establishment. Nature is apparently indifferent to the execution of many particular matters related to justice, such as the tallying of votes, the payment of debts and marriage rites. Nonetheless, the varying practices of human communities do not destroy the potential of natural justice any more than varying opinions about the shape of the earth disprove that it is a sphere.

Natural justice indeed has the same force and applicability universally, in all times and places. Its variability however makes it difficult to perceive. Whatever was just for Athens in the fourth century BC had as much natural basis as whatever is just for Boston at the beginning of the twenty-first century, but the requirements of natural justice for each differ. Nature issues no timeless maxims, precepts or laws for human beings to follow like it issues for the physical world.[8] Obligatory *and* variable, natural justice asks human beings to pay attention to their circumstances.

Although indeterminable a priori, specifications of natural justice, the first principles of ethics, are knowable because they are ontological; their variable specificity does not deny their ontological basis and therefore does not deny their knowability as such, either. Select human beings who have the faculty of intuition or *nous* apprehend natural justice and thereby recognize that in ethical matters human beings are obliged to heed certain truths; just as there are physical facts of nature so too there are ethical facts of nature.

The ontological element of justice makes it not only obligatory but also non-arbitrary or objective inasmuch as it is part of the ordered cosmos; what is right by nature for human beings harmonizes with the cosmos. It nonetheless becomes manifest only in the concrete. Part of what makes natural justice right for human beings is its inseparability from the particular. Aristotle offers no deductive a priori or hypothetical vantage point from which to ascertain a theory of justice because nature does not reduce the practical to the theoretical, or politics to physics.[9]

In other words, natural justice does not absolve human beings of choice-making. Indeed, nature gives us reason so that we can make the best, naturally right, choices for ourselves. Only we can discern, on the one hand, the leeway or possibilities nature grants and, on the other, the restrictions or limitations nature imposes, in any given situation.[10]

Human beings can realize natural justice by way of deliberate and conscious means, on the one hand, such as law and education, and by way of habitual and unconscious means, on the other, such as custom and social practices. The divine principle of nature works through the judgement of wise men who perceive the whole of nature and thus both the potential and the restrictions nature places on human beings, and who can influence law and education. Nature also makes that wisdom imperfectly available in the time-tested practices of custom.[11]

III NATURE AND THE UNITY OF THE ARISTOTELIAN CORPUS[12]

Related to the subject of Aristotle on natural justice and nature generally, is the disputed unity of his corpus. Aristotle wrote a number of works on a number of subjects and maintains that different degrees of precision are obtainable about each subject: physics, logic, biology and metaphysics surpass ethics, politics and rhetoric by that measure. At the same time, each subject implicates nature, indicating their connectedness or unity. Yet nature, by virtue of being itself a plurality, appears not to meet the requirement of knowability that Aristotle establishes in his logico-metaphysical works, namely, categorizability or classifiability: that which forms a class or category or a one is knowable.

Classes or categories of things are knowable or comprehensible because they each preserve distinctive forms or species. Because classes preserve different species, they constitute separate subjects of study or bodies of knowledge and thus require separate methods or sciences to be known: 'things which differ in genus have no means of passing into each other, and are more widely distant, and are not comparable' (*Met.* 1055a6).[13] As an unclassifiable plurality, nature seems to lack a science of its own and thus seems hopelessly unknowable, incomprehensible.

On the other hand, the very fact that Aristotle refers to nature, often frequently, in his various sorts of work, induces consideration of the nature of the natural plurality; for it appears to comprehend, join, or relate in some way the various branches of study. At least four features of the natural plurality provide grounds for relating or joining the various branches of study to one another: (1) its teleology or purposiveness, (2) its integration of form and matter, (3) its anthropocentricity and (4) its relation to unity.

First, Aristotle's view that nature ordains a purpose or end to each living thing is the basis on which he relates the generic branches of knowledge by analogy.[14] He illustrates in the *Politics* how the city – that which of all things would appear to be altogether conventional – is natural. Like any living organism, such as an acorn or a puppy, the city has a natural end, which is also, like the acorn's and puppy's ends, its most developed, mature and self-sufficient form. Political self-sufficiency is at least analogous to biological maturity, and the findings of the human or political sciences, on the one hand, and of the physical sciences, on the other, are accordingly analogous.

A second feature of the natural plurality, connected to its purposiveness, that appears to provide common ground for separate branches of study, is its composition by form and matter. If nature ordains purposes to living things, then it gives them principles or forms by which to realize those purposes. Forms, as the intelligible principles of material things, are immanent in matter. Matter and form as such have no antecedent reality; they exist together, by necessity. The form or intelligible principle immanent in the human body Aristotle calls soul. If, as Aristotle observes in *Nicomachean Ethics* I.13, the human soul is not only part reason and part desire, but part vegetative or bodily, then is not the study of the habits or functions of the body – namely, biology, relevant and not merely analogous to, the study of the habits of the soul – namely, ethics? If body and soul are one, then the habits of the 'body' must affect, and reflect, the habits of the 'soul', and vice versa. The 'body' cannot be in good condition or healthy unless the 'soul' is too, and vice versa.

A third characteristic of the natural plurality that would appear to join the human and physical sciences, and to confirm a link especially between biology and ethics, is its identification of man as the pinnacle of the hierarchy of living things. Since active reason characterizes only the human soul, man is a model of intelligibility in the realm of living things; if the intelligibility of all living things is relative to man's, then the attributes of non-human animals are not merely analogous, but comparable to, those of human beings.[15] In his *History of Animals*, Aristotle illustrates that the psychological traits, in particular, of nonhuman animals are comparable to man's; like man, they too have such qualities of character as courageousness, compassionateness and deceptiveness. The resemblance between the ways of the soul of man and those of animals suggests that the ways of the soul – the subject of ethics – are not simply products of human culture or nurture – not simply acquired or cultivated – but are to some extent given, in bodily nature. Indeed, if there is a bodily soul, then its study would seem to be most fittingly characterized not as ethics, but as bioethics, which the *History of Animals* seems to be.

A fourth feature of the natural plurality that provides grounds for relating the branches of study is its paradoxical relation to unity. In the same text in which Aristotle explains the principle of classification, which principle separates the bodies of knowledge, he also seems to explain indirectly the paradox of nature that would unify those branches. At the beginning of *Metaphysics*, Book X, he notes that all sets of contraries can be reduced to the primary or generic contraries of unity and plurality (*Met.* 1054a21–1055b29). Unity and plurality are contraries, or opposites, because unity is indivisible and plurality, divisible. The phenomenon of contrariety results from deprivation. Just as vice or badness is a privation of virtue or goodness, so odd is a privation of even. Thus, if unity and plurality are contraries, then plurality must be a privation of unity.

The privation of a category or class can result either in a contrary that forms a continuum with it, as virtue forms a continuum with vice, or in a contrary that constitutes a different class, as odd does from even. In the case of contraries that form a continuum, they share a substrate or common ground (*Met.* 1056a31–1056b1).

If nature is many, or indeed just two, then it is a plurality and the opposite of unity. That which is not one is a plurality. That nature is in one sense many is obvious, but also obvious according to Aristotle is that the substrate of nature is not one but two. Nature's duality is apparent from our own human constitution, which combines matter and form, the non-rational and rational. We are made aware of nature's duality by both our frustrations and our aspirations; the recognition that we are neither beasts nor gods, but rather in-between beings, gives rise to the perception that nature as we experience it is a privation of form, which is rational, from matter, which is non-rational. In that reflection itself, we glimpse the whole of nature; the truth about nature which lies in the realm of thought alone.

Indeed, Aristotle himself must have glimpsed the whole of nature in order to make the claim in the *Nicomachean Ethics* that the natural is that which has everywhere and always the same force or power (*NE* 1134b19–20). If the intellect can grasp or intuit the whole of nature, then the substrate or unity of nature must be a kind of intelligibility.

If nature as a whole is intelligible, if in other words the unity of nature is noetic, then surely the various branches of study – the biological, psychological, political, ethical and metaphysical, which focus independently on the physical, the human and the divine – must be in some way intelligible to and thus relevant to one another. By subsuming under the concept of nature not only the physical or empirical, as does post-Enlightenment thought, but also the human and the divine, Aristotle suggests that the physical, human and divine sciences are mutually relevant.

It seems, then, that nature does have its own appropriate method or science; if the whole of nature is knowable at all, then it is evidently so through that activity which apprehends both the demonstrable and the indemonstrable, namely philosophy.

CHAPTER 2

OVERVIEW OF THEMES

Identification of the themes of the *Politics*, and of the individual books in which those themes emerge and develop, relates to the matter of the intended order of the books, 'an area where all is hypothesis'.[1] Any hypothesis about the intended order generates temptation to make the text support the hypothesis. Pierre Pellegrin, for one, cautions against succumbing to that temptation: while one may legitimately have the conviction that a certain order of the books of the *Politics* makes sense, one should not regard that order as a proposition capable of sustaining an interpretation. One can end up, but not begin, with a thesis about the order of the books.[2] Likewise, as Carnes Lord states, 'an interpretation of the *Politics* . . . must depend importantly on the interpreter's view of the kind of work it is and the audience for which it was composed', but the interpreter must arrive at an understanding of the character of the *Politics* 'only by a comprehensive interpretation of the work as a whole'.[3] Any claims about the character and order of the books should be ventured on the basis of and substantiated by an analysis of its content.

More specifically, the presupposition of the interpretation put forth by this *Reader's Guide* challenges 'the old view that Books VII and VIII have been displaced from their proper position and belong between Books III and IV'[4] and the *reasons* given for the Jaegerian view that the books are in their proper order as they have come down to us. According to Werner Jaeger, Aristotle inserted Books IV–VI between Books III and VII to correct or mitigate the Platonic idealism of the flanking books (I–III and VII–VIII), which he had written earlier, when he was younger and more under the influence of Plato than when he was older and wrote his mature, original work.[5]

While it is plausible to maintain the present order of the books, as they have come down to us, as Aristotle's own original, intended, order, grounds for doing so that allege an intellectual development on the part of Aristotle are less convincing than grounds of a logical sequence of ideas. Books I–III concern two broad themes: the naturalness of the city, and the moral significance of the household. Within each of those themes are two subtopics. In discussing the naturalness of the city, Aristotle notes (a) the naturalness of ruling – rule creates the most advantageous relationships among members of a city – and (b) the difference between conventional or citizen virtue, and natural or full virtue, and the manifestation of that difference in correct and deviant regimes. In discussing the household, he makes clear that (a) private relationships and (b) private things, shared in public, are essential for the cultivation of moral virtue. Although the interpretation of this *Reader's Guide* does not contradict the general view that Books I–III cohere with Books VII and VIII in that they describe features of the best regime, it indicates that they are placed where they are, and apart from Books VII and VIII, because those features are features not only of the best regime but *also* of the best possible or second-best regime and of the lesser regimes described in the middle books.

More specifically, Books I–III argue that both rule and the household are essential features of any regime (i.e. viable regimes incorporate them) and that even overall deviant, defective regimes can maintain good or correct forms of ruling and the household.[6]

Books I–III, then, do not introduce simply 'a general theory of the state' (as Jaeger claims Book I does) or simply 'an ideal state' (as Jaeger claims Books II and III do) but rather the essential features of all regimes, including the best.[7] Thus the distinction between the best and second-best regimes is not as stark as Jaeger and others claim, and serves the lesson directed to legislators in the middle books, to preserve but also improve their regime. As P. A. Vander Waerdt explains,

the statesman will be guided by the double teleology which underlies the program of political science announced in iv: 1: his minimal aim will be the regime's preservation, but his higher aim will be to turn it toward the good life and *eudaimonia*, so much as circumstances permit . . . the purpose of the statesman's architectonic science is not merely to legislate in the interest of the regime in force . . . but to foster the good life and *eudaimonia* for others as far as possible through political virtue.[8]

To summarize with Harry V. Jaffa, it might be said that the line between the best and the lesser regimes is blurred because 'the best regime is the implicit subject of every book'.[9]

The unqualifiedly best regime then is neither purely speculative nor a blueprint for all regimes. Rather it serves to help legislators transform their own particular regime into an approximate form. The absolutely best form, the city 'one would pray for', can arise only if the proper equipment exists. Where the proper equipment does not exist, legislators should aim to bring about the best regime possible given the circumstances. Books VII and VIII then do not present an exclusive form of regime but a visionary perspective from which to judge all regimes; at the same time, if that form were to meet all its requisite circumstances, then it would become determinate and an actual regime.[10]

In sum, the present order of the books of the *Politics* instructs legislators, first, in Books I–III, about *essential* principles and features of regimes; second, in Books IV–VI, about myriad and sundry *contingencies*; and third, in Books VII and VIII, about *ideal* features and conditions.[11]

Now for discussion of themes without focus on the order of the books.

Turning now to a discussion of themes without focusing on the order of the books, we see that the dominant theme of the regime appears in every book by way of analysis of its parts and how they function. That alone would suggest a strictly empirical work, descriptive of past and present regimes, an inventory or catalogue akin to Aristotle's *The Athenian Constitution*. After introducing the subject of the regime in the first chapter, however, the second chapter introduces the theme of nature and a novel conception of it that links the city and its governance to nature through man: man is a *political* animal who thrives in cities and most of all in cities that achieve self-sufficiency. Cities are not only 'by nature' inasmuch as they fulfil man's animalistic needs, but 'according to nature' insofar as they fulfil man's political nature. Hence the first two chapters of the *Politics* raise the overriding question of the work: *What sort of regime fulfils man's political nature, or is self-sufficient?* They thereby establish that the *Politics* does not simply describe existing regimes but, by promising an answer to the question, prescribes improvements for them, if not also for future regimes. The co-dominant themes of 'regime' and 'nature' then indicate the inextricability of ethics and politics.

'Politics' occur because man's political nature is characterized chiefly not by his instinct to live with others but rather by his capacity for speech, meaning his ability to speak his mind about what he thinks is good and bad and just and unjust. When men come together out of a desire to procreate and survive, they speak their minds about how best to do so – how best to live. That leads to discussions about how best to organize themselves, govern themselves and spend their time. Hence it appears that the best regime would, at minimum, allow such discussions – in modern parlance – allow 'free speech'.

If the conditions of free speech are a function of the regime, then they are a function of convention: paradoxically, convention establishes the conditions for a regime according to nature. In other words, the naturalness of a regime requires the contribution of men. By including human nature, nature includes convention. Nature makes men partly responsible for the quality of their lives; it does not entirely determine it for them.

Nature, apart from human nature, nonetheless has some say over the quality of men's lives. It provides not only the natural resources available to every time and place in which men reside, but gives each human being his potential: every infant will become a man or a woman, and endowed with appetites, emotions and reason to different degrees depending on their sex and their individual make-up. By determining the potential of each individual, nature thereby determines the limitations of each.

Aristotle's decision to start the *Politics* by declaring the naturalness of the city indicates two points relevant to political practice: (1) because nature includes human nature, cities do not spring up without human effort and without human initiatives that reflect opinions about justice; human beings are responsible for such initiatives that affect the quality of life in a given city; and (2) although cities might appear to be strictly the result of human initiatives – that is, entirely man-made, conventional entities – nature limits their constellations; no law can turn men into women, or men into gods, for that matter. Human beings cannot create any sort of city they can imagine or wish for.

Together, these two points situate Aristotle's contribution to the history of ideas: namely, in between, on the one hand, the contributions of ancient poets and natural philosophers who attributed a city's fate to the Olympic Gods and saw nature as an entity distinct from the city, and, on the other, modern Enlightenment thought which pretends mastery or management of nature and thus autonomy over the city or the 'social contract'. The first point of view encourages passivity or mere prayer, the second, excessive control or overreaching. Human beings can shape their lives, but not entirely. They should take initiatives, but prudent ones, that consider possibilities and likely outcomes.

Aristotle's articulation of the naturalness of the city also establishes, more directly than does Plato, the aptness of the city for philosophical inquiry. If cities were simply conventional entities created entirely by the fancies of men, then they would be arbitrary, unyielding of timeless generalizations and insights into the human condition. Discussion about them would have no potential to teach us: to enable us to detect *reasons* for both failed and successful initiatives – why some policies work and others do not. If nature plays no role in political life, then no constancies or truths characterize it. Aristotle demonstrates, however, the opposite: reflection about various cities reveals commonalities. We can conclude certain truths about political life. Hence the city is a fruitful subject for philosophical thought.

As indicated, truths about political life involve capacities nature gives man, as well as limitations it imposes – or in other words, man's potential according to nature. The realization of that potential generates division between public and private spaces and activities – another theme woven throughout the *Politics*. More specifically, constellations of attributes among human beings – men, women, children, natural slaves, those with stellar leadership capabilities, those with philosophic acuity, the aged and so on – generate households, political offices of various rank, common farms, leisured discussion and priesthoods.[12]

Moreover, the attributes of a given population largely determine the form of regime they live under, whether kingship, aristocracy, polity, democracy, oligarchy or tyranny. In the middle books (IV–VI) of the *Politics*, Aristotle thoroughly discusses the advantages and disadvantages of each of those six types, as well as variations of them, with respect to the aim of living well. In other words, he follows up his opening question, *What sort of regime fulfils man's political nature, or is self-sufficient?*, with an analysis of regime types.

That analysis generates additional themes and questions: qualifications for citizenship (birth? geography? political participation?); the rule of men versus the rule of law (Does a city require both? Is one or the other necessarily a better means to justice?); reason and wilfulness (How does their dynamic affect politics? Is 'the will of the people' a good navigator for a ship of state?); virtue and freedom (Should government make one or the other a priority? Can political arrangements render virtue and freedom complementary?); change versus the status quo (Is all change progress? Is tradition a good political guide?); political action and philosophic contemplation (Does a good regime incorporate both? Should philosophy inform rule? If so, how so?); and, related to the last, education (What are the best means? And what, its end?).

CHAPTER 3

READING THE TEXT

Politics I

INTRODUCTION

The first book of the *Politics* brings to our attention and illuminates a key paradox: namely that a city is both a single whole and a plurality of parts. If we understand why a city is at once one and many, then we are abler to maintain cities. Aristotle thereby implies a connection between knowledge and practice.

The paradoxical character of the city generates not only questions but also answers fundamental to knowledge of it. A preliminary methodological question – how to investigate or study that which is simultaneously single and plural – leads to answers that explain why the city can, should and in fact must, be studied. What appears to be impossible turns out to be mandatory, because the parts of a city include human beings, and human beings question how they live; the critical faculty of human beings, reason or speech, not only divides but unites citizens. The divided or complex unity of the city is thus natural because human beings are endowed by nature with reason or speech.

In addition to the methodological problem, Book I addresses a host of problems concerning one particular part of the city, namely the household. The household is an especially problematic part of the city because it is itself a composition of parts. Composed of a man, a woman, children and slaves, a household confronts a functional dilemma similar to that of the city: how to maintain its character as a discrete entity. Although discussion of the relationships between husband and wife, between parents and children, and between masters and slaves appear to dominate Book I, two additional, albeit related, subjects – namely, ruling and money-making – are also given serious, if more concentrated, treatment. Concerned then with government, the economy and the household, Book I addresses matters germane to all cities.

The organization of the book highlights the overarching importance of the connection between the city's unity and its parts through nature. For Aristotle shows in the first two chapters that the compound unity of the city results from the spontaneous or natural desire of human beings to live and to live well. Self-preservation, reproduction and self-sufficiency are ends given by nature. Although nature also gives us means to realize those ends, no means guarantee their realization. Indeed, the chief means of realization nature gives us, reason, which Aristotle discusses in the second chapter, makes clear nature's intention: it's up to us to figure out how to survive and to live well. Hence in the remainder of Book I and of the *Politics* Aristotle gives us extensive advice, based on observations, about how to do that. His discussion from the third chapter to the end of Book I about household management, ruling more generally, and business expertise thus responds to the book's beginning focal point: nature's mandate.

I. 1

In the opening sentence of the *Politics*, Aristotle indicates his subject and the method of investigation it requires: to learn about the city we must observe it. We must proceed empirically and reason inductively, from particular observations. Aristotle begins by observing that the city is a union or partnership, and like all other partnerships inasmuch as it aims at some good. But it is unique in that it includes them. That being the case, the good the city aims at is superior to the good aimed at by other partnerships; the city is evidently responsible for allowing other partnerships to form and to function – that is *its* function or purpose. Aristotle thus indicates, first, that any conclusions reached in the following inquiry about the city are drawn from what appears or is evident to us; second, because the city is inclusive of all other partnerships, it cannot be understood apart from an understanding of those partnerships; and third, because human partnerships appear to be motivated by some good, inquiry into the city, the political partnership, and its constitutive partnerships, entails inquiry into the good, or ethics. That is to say, we cannot observe human engagement without evaluating it.

The remainder of the opening passage amplifies the observation that a city is constituted of parts, by claiming that its parts require different forms of rule, and thus that an investigation of its parts will illuminate those different forms, which are political rule, kingly rule, household management and mastery.

I. 2

Chapter 2 is the most important chapter of the *Politics* because it presents the surprising claim that the city is natural. What could be more conventional – more man-made – than the city?

Aristotle begins the chapter by depicting the origins of the city and its stages of development, as if to suggest that the city exists by nature because it grows or evolves like a physical organism. Although the account appears initially to be a chronological one, similar to state-of-nature accounts found in later political theories, it turns out to be rather a *purposive* account. That is to say, it explains *why* each of the component parts of a city exists; the best understanding of human partnerships indeed derives from a study of their origins, but the true origins are the motivations of those involved. Every development can be traced to the desired aims of persons.

Let us now consider the developmental account, which comprises the first half of the chapter. Two pairs of persons need one another to fulfil aims that are not deliberately chosen but rather spontaneously desired. Male and female need one another to reproduce, and persons with foresight but not bodily strength and those with the latter but not the former need one another to survive. Because reproduction and self-preservation are ends that a single human being desires but is inadequately constituted to achieve, human beings do not live alone in the wilderness.

If foresight is characteristic of some persons and bodily strength of others then, Aristotle reasons, the former are more suited to rule and the latter to be ruled. Here Aristotle introduces his concepts of natural master and natural slave, which he will elaborate in chapters 4–7.

The existence of men and women and masters and slaves testifies to nature's generosity, insofar as they are means tailored to satisfy necessity. Each type of constitution serves one primary function rather than many functions. As Aristotle points out, only barbarians or those lacking the ability to rule fail to distinguish the labour of childbirth from other physical labour – they treat all females as slaves.

Two partnerships constituted for the sake of necessity, then, those between a man and a woman and between a master and a slave, generated the household. The claim does not aspire to historical truth, for Aristotle at once notes Hesiod's observation that poor households own oxen instead of slaves; the point and timeless truth is rather that households form to fulfil basic wants. Human beings want to have children and provisions.

A union of households is a village. Villages arise naturally but are not formed out of necessity: they are the extended families of households, or clans, and do not satisfy basic desires. Because villages are not vital and only the necessary consequence of households they are not *intentionally formed* – perhaps the reason Aristotle seldom mentions them again in the *Politics*. He does say here that villages meet non-daily needs and, although he does not specify what those needs are and how they are met, he likely means that goods and tools are borrowed and shared – which he identifies later as a feature of a good economy.

Before Aristotle all but abandons the subject of the village, he makes two historical claims. The first being that kings were originally simply the eldest member of a clan; the tradition of kingship derived from the authority structure of the village. Ancient peoples thus committed a mistake Aristotle sets out in chapter 1 to correct: namely, the assumption that ruling a small city is no different from ruling a large household. The second historical claim Aristotle makes here also divorces from a traditional way of thinking but is more remarkable because it challenges man's conception of the Gods. Because ancient peoples lived under kings, Aristotle says, they asserted that the Gods have kings too. Men thus make another mistake, Aristotle implies, when they anthropomorphize the divine.

Aristotle's discussion of the village paradoxically accomplishes a lot while deflating its subject. By observing that villages are by-products of households and not animated as they are by spontaneous individual desires, Aristotle highlights the vitality of the household by comparison. The discussion also explains chapter 1's reference to large households and, by suggesting that the village largely serves to facilitate exchange, it eliminates it as the proper focus of an inquiry into the problem of rule. While the village may be irrelevant to understanding the city, Aristotle hints, just before leaving the subject and turning to the city as a whole, that a correct conception of the divine may not be irrelevant.

A union of several villages, that is complete, is a city. By 'complete' Aristotle means self-sufficient and by 'self-sufficient' he means equipped to foster living well. Because the city is the end of partnerships that satisfy needs, it does so too, but it is more than the sum of its parts, and its character more than that of its foundations. The nature of a city is no more that of its fundamental partnerships than is the nature of a man that of a child, or the nature a family that of a slave. Nature brings about the best; the good life is better than mere life.

How does nature bring about the best? By enlisting human beings who, as both shaped by and shapers of the city, are thus 'political' by nature. One who is uncultivated by family and law is either vulgar and aggressive or divine, and one who does not speak in some fashion and thereby contribute to the city is not human. That our political nature concerns our capacity for speech more than an instinct to associate or be together Aristotle indicates by contrasting us to bees and herd animals. In other words, we are not simply or foremost social.

Indeed the function of speech indicates a potential for conflict as well as for cooperation, by asserting our perceptions of good and bad, and just and unjust. Because we are by nature beings who judge, judgements characterize our intentional partnerships – households and cities. Households and cities therefore may or may not be, as we know, harmonious.

Aristotle's elaboration of his contention that the city is the end of the household continues to preserve the integrity of the household as such, as well as that of the individual as such, by pointing out only that the latter cannot be conceived – and therefore, he implies, properly discussed or analysed – without reference to the city. The city is conceptually 'prior by nature' to the household and individuals because they function in connection to it, as a foot or hand functions in connection to a body; the city as such – rightly conceived – does not undermine their integrity or homogenize their unique status because each of them has its own peculiar animus and end essential to the functioning of the whole city. Aristotle thus makes clear that while the parts are dependent on the whole, the whole is dependent on its parts. While human beings are neither solitary beasts nor earthly gods, sufficient unto themselves, cities are not magically self-sufficient without the contributions of their dynamic parts.

Aristotle closes his analysis of the naturalness of the city with further juxtapositions. Although we have an impulse to form cities, he says, huge credit should go the person who first constituted one, denying again that social instinct is politically foundational or paramount. We are indebted to that unidentified person because without law and administration of justice human beings are the worst of all animals because of their very capacities to create law and administer justice, which capacities they can employ for opposite ends. Unless law and justice cultivate human beings to virtue, they are the most unholy and most savage of beings – the most indulgent of all in sex and food. The modern reader can consider the truth of this contention with reference to both ancient and contemporary cultures, from Roman debauchery to global sex trafficking. Can the character of a city, as determined by its laws and administration of justice, not only correct but even prevent such behaviour?

Aristotle's analysis of the genesis and nature of the city in chapter 2 suggests a number of implications. It implies above all that we modern readers must suspend our conception of nature as governed by fixed laws that forecast events, and not by ends ordaining physical and moral requirements. Nature not only ordains a colt to become a horse, but also a man to become political and a city to become self-sufficient. Human nature or initiative attests that nature does nothing in vain, furnishing means to the achievement of its ends. Those means guarantee those ends insofar as the latter include the exercise of the former – that is, insofar as nature ordains man to exercise his judgement. Men can nonetheless judge poorly and contravene nature by creating conventions that thwart justice and living well. Man-made practices and institutions do not necessarily serve the best ends.

In other words, although nature includes human nature, human nature is characterized by judgement that may or may not perceive the physical and moral requirements of a good life, the end ordained by nature. Hence not all ways of life created by man are good, or according to nature.

By claiming that nature sanctions human judgement as requisite to cities, Aristotle frees them from divine control; the contemporary Greek view of cities as divinely ordained or protected by the Gods is replaced with a conception of them as products of human endeavour. Cities are not at the mercy, or in the laps, of the Gods. Prayer and sacrifice are not enough. While Aristotle boldly challenges traditional ancient beliefs and moves towards ideas characteristic of modern political thought, he does not run the whole nine yards to a social contract theory of the state by granting us complete authority or freedom over the city and asserting that consent alone establishes legitimacy or the best way of life. Rather, by revealing nature's ends, he charges human freedom with responsibility to those ends. We bear responsibility for the character of cities, and nature obliges us to make them good, just and self-sufficient by making us political or judgemental creatures.

To state differently, Aristotle suggests both possibility and limitation. Human perceptions of good and bad and just and unjust yield innovations of varying duration, indicative of their suitability to the human condition; we discover that we cannot live any way we like. Nature constrains us individually and collectively. Our different personal constitutions make us dependent on one another as well as inclined towards independence; our capacity to judge gives us grounds for agreement as well as for disagreement. Nature also at once constrains and frees us by inducing the desire and means to live well without telling us how to do so.

By challenging us with freedom and constraints to live the best possible life, nature dignifies the city. Our unconstrained free choice or creativity cannot fashion a city worthy of human beings. A city must heed both low and high nature, both our impulses and our aspirations. The task of politics, Aristotle thus suggests at the outset of the *Politics*, is not an easy one.

Debate over whether Aristotle is an idealist or a realist thus shirks obligations that the complexity of nature imposes on us. On the one hand, if nature ordains human fulfilment through self-sufficient cities and does nothing in vain, then we should be confident about the prospect of a good life. On the other hand, if human beings are essentially impulsive or licentious and aggressive, then we should anticipate constant turbulence. Emphasis on the first claim relaxes us (we will likely live well); emphasis on the second discourages us (conflict is here to stay). Aristotle is not however making a prognosis. Rather, he reveals the umbrella of nature over human nature in order to explain why the inventions or products of human nature – the largest being the city – *can*, *should* and *must* be questioned or examined. Characterized by the active speech or judgement characteristic of human nature, the city is naturally self-critical: it cannot evade the question, how should its members live? Not only does the city contain the means, the will and the mandate to question itself, but also the experiences from which to derive answers to the questions it poses. We are back to Aristotle's first instruction: to observe. Answers to how best to live are available if we observe or contemplate our experiences; successes and failures direct us to nature's ends. We can increase our prospect for the good life nature ordains and pre-empt the turbulence nature allows if we reflect on our experiences and act accordingly. Aristotle's presentation of the naturalness of the city predicts neither our success nor our failure in that enterprise, but rather shows that that enterprise, which is on the first order reflective or philosophical, is possible.

Aristotle's point then is twofold: not only is the goodness or authority as such of any given city in our hands, but its recognition or determination is a function of philosophical reflection. Only philosophy, not the city or politics as such, can determine whether or not a city fulfils nature's end of self-sufficiency. By presenting the naturalness of the city then, Aristotle invites his audience to contemplate that end and the means vital to its attainment. If that invitation paradoxically suggests that political philosophy, and not politics or the city as such, is the most authoritative means by which to complete human life, then it also implies that the best city is friendly to that insight.

I. 3

Aristotle devotes the remaining eleven chapters of Book I to the household and its management. While the extent of his attention to these subjects indicates their importance, the placement of his attention to them verifies the indispensability of households to the city as such, since Book I introduces the subject of the city in general. That is, as shown in chapter 2, a city by definition includes households or, as Aristotle observes at the start of chapter 3, every city is composed of households.

Because the household is itself a composite, household management is not a single art or form of rule. The parts of the household are not however, as they might seem to be, reducible to the members per se of the household, but rather to their roles: namely, master, slave, husband, wife, father and children. Those roles imply a manner of relation or bearing to their counterparts. A manner of bearing constitutes a kind of expertise or responsiveness. The roles identified indicate three kinds of expertise or mutual relations: mastery, marital relations and rule over children. Aristotle observes that his language lacks a precise word for the relationship between a man and a woman, implying that their union in marriage does not itself convey a dynamic, or respective manners of bearing. Similarly, the status in the Greek text for the word conveying 'rule over children' is uncertain: Aristotle may mean either paternal or parental rule. Although paternal rule is consistent with his identification of the role of father to the exclusion of that of mother, Aristotle notes again that his language lacks a precise term for the kind of rule he means, lending support to a notion of parental rule, since the word for paternal rule, *patrike*, was available. Because both of these admitted linguistic difficulties concern members of the household having one attribute in particular in common – namely, their status as free persons (rather than as slaves) – they suggest the direction, as well as the novelty, of Aristotle's analysis: relations between free persons in the household call for investigation because they are not properly conceived, and thus captured by specific Greek terms. Conversely, the term 'mastery' – *despotike* in the Greek – is linguistically evocative – of despotic domination. Yet Aristotle says that mastery too needs discussion, thus perhaps that evoked sense is misleading. In any case, he says that he will determine what each of the three household relationships *ought to be*.

That determination requires consideration of another obvious part of household management: the art of acquisition, or business expertise (for without possessions it is impossible either to live or live well, Aristotle notes). Who should provide for the household, and to what end? Aristotle thus sets the stage for his substantial discussion of slavery.

I. 4–7

For historical and political reasons, Aristotle's discussion of slavery has become perhaps the most well-known and controversial part of the *Politics*. Whether or not he deserves his reputation as a defender of practices commonly associated with slavery the reader can decide, but not judiciously without consideration of Aristotle's empirical observations and the theoretical generalizations he derives from them. Because the latter, concentrated mostly in chapter 5, are central not only to his conception of the master–slave relationship but also to his conception of other forms of rule discussed throughout the *Politics*, they are the focus of the following commentary.

Chapter 4 presents matter-of-fact or unarguable definitions of 'slave' and 'master': a slave is an owned animate instrument of action (as distinguished from an owned inanimate instrument of production, such as a loom or a coffeemaker); a master is an owner of a slave. If a slave is owned, then he does not belong to himself, from which Aristotle concludes that a slave is a human being 'who does not belong to himself by nature', thereby suggesting that the slave's status as a possession is a consequence or manifestation of his nature. In chapter 5, Aristotle begins to explain *why* certain human beings do not belong to themselves by nature.

He says – in one of the most important and scientifically prescient paragraphs of the *Politics* – that the answer is not difficult to discern, either philosophically or empirically. For if we observe and think about the world in which we live, we see not only the phenomenon of 'ruling and being ruled' or, in a word, hierarchies, but the necessity and benefits of that phenomenon or of those hierarchies. We see the necessity in the inferior and superior qualities of beings: mother tigers drag their cubs out of harm's way into safe dens, for example, ensuring their preservation. We see the benefits of rule in the complementariness of beings: a horse can pull a cart for a man, while a man can remove a stone from the horse's hoof. We can also discern better and worse forms of rule, the quality of rule always being dependent on the quality of that which is ruled: a dog that bites, a toddler that hits and a man that robs, require different treatment from those that don't. Better natures and conduct elicit better rule. The activity of ruling thus functionally connects the ruler and ruled; how each functions depends on the other. This is true Aristotle says, in a sentence that anticipates modern physics, whether the ruling and the ruled either constitute a whole or are discrete parts, and whether they are either animate or inanimate. While the phenomenon of rule is easiest to observe among discrete animate beings – that is, among animals and human beings, it is intrinsic to such inanimate wholes as musical harmonies. That is, notes create music by ruling over and being ruled by other notes. Aristotle stops this line of argument to stay focused, but mentions another sort of inquiry that would extend it, suggesting perhaps a science that explores other inanimate wholes – such as rocks – held together by some form of rule, or forces.

Having discussed rule between separate beings and within an inanimate whole, Aristotle turns to rule within an animate whole – within one living being. He does so apparently because a single living being most obviously manifests rule according to nature, or the difference between good rule and bad rule. A living being in the best state exemplifies a naturally good relationship between its superior and inferior parts when its soul rules its body. By contrast, a depraved state reflects bad and unnatural rule, the body ruling the soul. Aristotle then makes clear that by the 'best state' he does not mean simply physical health; the soul too has its superior and inferior parts that have a proper natural relation – namely when the intellect rules the passions. These claims, advanced and associated with happiness by Aristotle in *The Nicomachean Ethics*, are central to his political philosophy because they establish criteria for superiority and inferiority, the justification for all kinds of rule.

Aristotle foreshadows as much in this context by noting again that the manner of ruling reflects the nature or quality of the ruled: the soul rules a body with the rule characteristic of a master, while the intellect or part of the soul having reason rules over the passionate part with political and kingly rule. We have yet to learn about all the forms of rule, but Aristotle underscores that superior should rule inferior in every case – human beings should rule animals, males, females and generally better human beings should rule lesser human beings – because nature establishes that norm. The political relevance of nature is incontrovertible.

If nature makes some human beings as different from others as souls are from bodies or as men are from beasts, then they should be ruled accordingly. That is, if the best work that can come from them is physical labour, then they are slaves by nature and should be treated as such – for their own good. Making explicit his earlier suggestion that a slave belongs to another human being because he is capable of belonging to another – or is in other words incapable of self-direction, Aristotle adds that a natural slave can follow but does not himself have, reason. Aristotle thus presents the slave's welfare – not the need for physical labour – as the paramount justification for mastery. Indeed, he notes that the need for slaves scarcely differs from the need for domesticated animals: both can do physical work.

Scholars debate whether or not Aristotle has now contradicted himself, since chapter 2 identified speech or reason (*logos*) as a defining attribute of man. Some scholars even allege that the contradiction is intentionally ironic: if slaves by nature lack reason, then there are no human beings who are natural slaves – Aristotle's implied point. Another tack focuses slavishness on a dispositional inclination to follow rather than to direct or lead; a slave's passivity either deactivates reason or manifests its impairment – that is, is either cause or symptom of his mental deficiency. A thorough resolution of the debate might derive from an analysis of the kinds or dimensions of reason as well as of states of soul that Aristotle identifies in his many treatises. Nonetheless, a perhaps satisfactory present resolution focuses on the correction of popular views Aristotle apparently wants to accomplish: natural slaves ought to be treated humanely, whether or not they are technically, or politically, human beings. That is, they ought to be treated like human beings insofar as their slavish qualities allow or, more precisely, because of their slavish qualities: to direct them is to answer their need to be directed.

Consistent with that interpretation, Aristotle says that the identification of natural slaves is not necessarily easy. Although human beings lacking reason or initiative may or may not be prevalent – Aristotle testifies only to their existence – they do not always appear different from other men. When nature's intention is realized, human beings deficient in reason have strong bodies suited to menial tasks, and those who are sufficiently reasonable have bodies suited for civic life, chiefly political office and military service. But often robust men are also reasonable, agile and apt for leadership, and often men of ordinary build or small stature, incapable of self-discipline and initiative. Why the opposite of nature's apparent intention often results Aristotle does not say. But by noting that the matter of who should be slaves and who masters would be easily solved if some men looked like Gods, he induces two compatible thoughts: no obligation to human beings inheres in nature, and the difficulties nature presents inspire human beings to oblige themselves. Nature not only fails to fashion some men in the image of Gods, so that we can gladly serve them, but also fails to make the beauty of souls as obvious as the beauty of bodies, so that we can easily identify who is naturally superior. Yet evidence that some persons are naturally slavish and others naturally free encourages the latter to benefit the former and render them more useful by way of mastery.

In other words, the existence of natural slaves encourages the practice of slavery. Not all slavery is just however. Aristotle makes that clear in chapter 6, where he lays out three positions, two of which defend the practice of slavery and the third opposes it. One defence of slavery holds that spoils of war, including human captives, legally belong to the victors. Opponents of that convention argue that neither superior force nor anything else can justify enslavement, because justice consists in mutual kindness. Aristotle points out truth in both views: might per se does not equal right but might backed by virtue, exerted over inferiors, does. Moreover, even proponents of the first view admit that the origin of war is not always just and that enemies in war can include men of the highest rank, not suited for slavery. By admitting that not all prisoners of war deserve enslavement, they are seeking, Aristotle says, 'the slave by nature'. They presuppose, in other words, that some persons are well born and virtuous by nature and others not, and in essence concur with Aristotle's position that only the latter merit enslavement.

Aristotle himself admits nonetheless that like does not always beget like; the respective offspring of slaves and masters do not necessarily merit the circumstances of their parents. If nature does not predictably fulfil its apparent intention, then we must rely on human judgement to discern who deserves to be enslaved. If we judge well, then everyone will benefit; masters and slaves will even become friends of a sort.

Although discernible characteristics establish master–slave relationships, the respective conduct of masters and slaves defines the work or function proper to each, implying a science of slavery and a science of mastery. Slaves perform chores, some more necessary than others, such as cooking. Mastery is the ability to command slaves, not a dignified undertaking, Aristotle says, apparently because it oversees the merely necessary business of life. If possible then a free man should hire an overseer for his slaves, so that he can engage in politics or philosophy. He should not however delegate the obligation to procure his slaves, because again that requires the perception of a free man. Aristotle thus closes his discussion of slavery with the suggestion that its just practice is a condition of politics and philosophy (the first mention of 'philosophy' in the *Politics*); natural slaves should do immediately necessary work so that their natural superiors can do other important work. Hence if the welfare of natural slaves is the first, effective cause or justification of the institution of slavery, then politics and philosophy are its end or final cause.

I. 8–11

In the next four chapters, Aristotle continues to address the general question of Book I, What is according to nature for human beings?, and the more specific question, What is according to nature in the constitution of the household and its management? Having discussed the subject of the household's animate possessions in chapter 7, Aristotle moves on in chapter 8 to the subject of inanimate possessions, or material goods. Does household management include not only their use, but also their acquisition? Are there some modes of acquiring or generating wealth that are natural and others that are unnatural? Do answers to those questions hold lessons for the city?

Aristotle argues over the next four chapters that acquisition of wealth is not the same as but is subordinate to household management, that some modes of acquisition are more natural than others, and that the natural or good material condition of the household is instructive for the city. In doing so he presents three more pairs of contrasts: Just as he differentiated natural slavery from conventional or unnatural slavery, he differentiates natural from unnatural ways of acquiring wealth, natural from unnatural amounts of wealth, and even natural from unnatural uses of money. Ultimately he suggests that both households and cities should be naturally wealthy, or self-sufficient.

Aristotle sets out by arguing that the art of acquisition, as a means of bringing to the household the goods it needs to function, assists household management. But many forms of acquisition exist, and determine ways of life, such as farming and nomadism – the two most common – and hunting, piracy and fishing. Because these forms either generate or gather goods, they are to be distinguished from barter and commerce, which merely give and receive them. If a single mode of acquisition from land or sea is inadequate for self-sufficiency, persons sometimes successfully combine two or more other modes to achieve it. Nature assists the goal of self-sufficiency by giving human beings animals for use and sustenance, and giving animals plants for their use and sustenance. Nonetheless war – inasmuch as it encompasses hunting animals as well as acquiring human beings 'suited to be ruled but unwilling' – is a natural form of acquisitive expertise. By advising the free man to procure his own slaves, Aristotle already indicated in chapter 7 that this second kind of just war is part of household management.

The physical resources and hierarchies nature provides fulfil the needs of the household as well as needs of the city more generally. Forms of acquisition that follow nature's cues thus seem to generate true wealth, limited naturally by availability and by needs. If limited wealth or self-sufficiency characterizes the good life, then household managers and political rulers alike should not strive for material goods beyond that limit. By contradicting the poet Solon on this subject, Aristotle illustrates that poetry does not always convey wisdom or good advice. Unlimited pursuit of wealth is a decidedly unpoetic way of life.

Nonetheless, money and commerce were reasonable developments, Aristotle says. For they derive from barter or exchange which itself derives from need. While there is no need for exchange within a household because goods are used for specific purposes, there is such need among them to replenish or maintain those goods, reminding us of the rationale given earlier for the village, to meet non-daily needs. Once foreigners began importing necessary goods and exporting surplus, money was devised and commerce replaced exchange. Over time, through experience, commerce became the art of making a profit, which divorced money from need or natural sufficiency. Apparently then money can circulate naturally or simply conventionally; money circulated for profit is worthless because it is useless for necessary things. A rich man, like Midas, can starve. Lots of money is not natural or true wealth.

The utility of money and commerce for natural sufficiency is paradoxically the origin of their abuse. We need them to bring goods into the city and to facilitate exchange among households, but they can be directed to the accumulation of money. Just as gluttony stems from the fact that we need some food and cannot abstain from eating, commerce for profit stems from the fact that we need some things to live and cannot abstain from commerce to obtain them. But by way of an investigation of the arts Aristotle shows that, just as eating is not the cause of gluttony, commerce is not the cause of unnecessary accumulations of money.

The cause of course is desire. For every art is limited by its end. Health limits the art of medicine; once a wound is healed or a cold cured, there is no further need to apply a poultice or drink an elixir. The same could be said of wealth and the art of commerce except that wealth, unlike health, has two forms, namely sufficiency and superfluity (though a similar dichotomy with respect to health has emerged with the invention of cosmetic surgery). Accordingly, there are two different arts, one productive of each end. Commercial or business expertise productive of natural wealth and that productive of money are again very close and often confused (like eating and gluttony) because money (like food) is a means common to both. Consequently some persons think that the art of household management is to increase money or even just to hold on to it. The purpose of money, however, is to use it for useful things. Desire unsatisfied by sufficiency misuses business expertise to circulate money for the sake of more money. Money and business expertise are thus not themselves blameworthy or the root of all evil.

Indeed, when desire for money takes over, those who fail to accumulate money through business expertise try other arts, corrupting them as well: some actors act, some writers write, some doctors practice medicine and some generals lead wars, in order to get rich. Misdirecting their courage, initiative and energy to the goal of money, they undermine their work, integrity and self-confidence. As if money were the end of life, they are serious about living, but not about living well.

Since living well is the end of both households and cities, lessons about household management pertain to political rule. Like household managers, political rulers too should make use of business expertise. The proper and natural use of money and commerce provides things that households and cities need to live well. By tailoring management of their respective economies to their obligation to promote living well, households and cities use money according to nature, as a means to an end.

It appears nonetheless true that households and cities can live more, or less, according to nature. That complication, underlying Aristotle's discussion of household and political economies, crystallizes in chapter 11. Although the chapter focuses on the practical knowledge various modes of acquisition require, it complicates the naturalness of those modes – in part by introducing another one, and in part by ranking the sorts of work they involve. At the outset of the discussion in chapter 8, acquisition from the land is said to be the most natural mode of acquisition, and commerce the least natural. The first requires knowledge about the cultivation of crops and the care of animals, the second knowledge about transporting and selling cargo, money-lending and wage labour – the last done by artisans and physical labourers. But chapter 11 introduces a third art of acquisition or business expertise and says that it falls in between agriculture and commerce on the spectrum of naturalness: namely, harvesting things from the earth, chiefly lumbering and mining. Likewise the practical knowledge involved is partly similar to that needed in agriculture and partly to that needed in commerce. Although the way of life most natural to man still seems to be that closest to the land, Aristotle complicates that conclusion by characterizing the work involved in the three modes of acquisition.

The best sort of work requires the most skill; it can afford least to leave matters to chance. The most vulgar sort damages the body most. The most slavish sort relies most on physical strength. And the most ignoble, sorts of work that are least in need of virtue or goodness. Hence the sort of work that is best for man is that which most preserves his mind and his body.

The relative naturalness of the three modes of acquisition to the life of man does not evidently correspond to their use of the land or their proximity to the natural environment. While farming, mining and lumberjacking require skill and minimizing hazards such as weather, they also require physical labour that risks injury. And while commerce or trafficking goods requires labour to transport cargo, it also calls on skill to manufacture goods and to manage money. In fact, Aristotle notes that while plenty of handbooks about agriculture exist, more on business are needed. Furthermore, in addition to business smarts, does not the management of money in particular require considerable virtue or goodness, at least if it serves the end of sufficiency rather than superfluity?

As if to confirm that the management of money requires both intelligence and good character, including gumption or courage, Aristotle recounts an anecdote about Thales of Miletus, a man who, when he was chided for his poverty, made use of his scientific knowledge to make a lot of money, thereby proving that he could, but did not want to spend his life doing so.

Knowing how to make a lot of money fast is useful – to households and even more so to cities, Aristotle says. Political rulers should have that sort of practical knowledge to raise revenues; some in government even appropriately concern themselves exclusively with it.

While the specifics of that knowledge are not germane to the immediate inquiry, the fact that it is necessary is germane. For it helps establish two points: money-making should not be a priority, but also, it should not be eschewed. If all households and cities did was to raise money, then presumably they would not have any need to know how to raise it fast. At the same time, the stark alternatives presented by the example of Thales, between a life devoted to the pursuit of knowledge lived in poverty, and one devoted to making a quick buck, make us wonder if they are the only alternatives. Indeed Aristotle notes that although the business scheme Thales devised was attributed to his knowledge of astronomy (enabling him to predict a good harvest and rent out all the available olive presses in advance), the principle of monopoly is business expertise that is universally available. If political rulers and household managers alike readily commanded such business expertise, then perhaps they could avoid the need to make money fast.

Thus Aristotle's discussion of modes of acquisition begins in chapter 8 by suggesting that limited wealth in the form of goods generated by agriculture promotes a good life, and ends in chapter 11 by suggesting that a reserve of wealth in the form of money generated by commerce does. In between he reveals that the question of what mode of acquisition is best or most natural for man requires consideration of his constitution as a whole and his proper end. But before that he showed that not all human beings are identically constituted and thus have different ends or functions. Evidently then which mode of acquisition is best depends on the characteristics of the populace in question.

I. 12–13

Having discussed at length the economies of the household and the city, which began with an analysis of the master–slave relationship, Aristotle turns in the last two chapters of Book I to the other two relationships constituting the household, namely that between husband and wife and that between parents and children. Although between naturally free individuals, they are nonetheless also, like the master–slave relationship, characterized by rule, as are all relationships according to nature, as already argued. The question is, what sort of rule, in each case?

Aristotle reasons that rule over children is kingly because kings, superior in some respect to but from the same people as their subjects, rule them benevolently. Inasmuch as age establishes relative maturity or development, it marks inferiority and superiority. While seniority in age establishes the superiority of both mothers and fathers over their children, Aristotle again, as earlier, does not mention the former and moreover here speaks only of paternal rule and kings – not of maternal rule and queens. The question of whether fathers alone exercise kingly rule draws attention to Aristotle's characterizations of male and female and of the relationship between husband and wife.

Aristotle declares that the male, unless constituted against nature, is better at leading than the female and should therefore lead in marriage, in a way consistent with political rule, in which ruler and ruled differ in presentation, formalities and privileges, regardless of whether or not they are equal by nature and alternate ruling and being ruled. Natural differences between men and women however extend beyond the capacity for leadership to all the virtues, moral and intellectual.

Moreover, the virtues of each member of the household differ from those of the others, a fact pivotal to its good management, Aristotle says. Hence he devotes chapter 13 to their enumeration and analysis.

The virtues of men, women, slaves and children differ because the constitution of their souls differs. Lacking a deliberative element, a slave displays virtue chiefly by way of discipline and dedication to his work. Similarly, the undeveloped deliberative capacity of a child allows only sporadic self-command. By contrast, a woman has a developed deliberative capacity but it does not always command her like a man's deliberative capacity always tends to command him, which affects her display of the moral virtues, such as moderation, courage and justice. Hence Aristotle concludes that virtue in general is not best defined, as some have defined it, as a good condition of the soul or as acting correctly, but rather as a number of different virtues.

Household management therefore entails instilling various virtues in or eliciting them from, different members of the household. Stating that the master should instil virtue even in his slaves and not merely instruct them in their work, Aristotle rehabilitates the dignity of mastery somewhat from his earlier account. Most importantly he argues, mentioning education for the first time in the *Politics*, that the function of the household is education. Pointing out that women are half of the free persons in a city, and children are its future citizens, Aristotle perhaps suggests a role for mothers; while they do not lead their children in the way fathers do, their own unique virtues may help develop, if not the intellectual virtues of their children, then their moral virtues. In any case, the excellence of a city depends on the excellence of its women and children.

STUDY QUESTIONS

1. What requires investigation in order to understand the manner in which a city should be ruled?
2. What does Aristotle mean by the claim that the city exists by nature?
3. Why is man a political animal?

Why does Aristotle begin his work with the argument that the city is natural?

Why are there slaves and masters?

Does Aristotle defend the practice of slavery? Why or why not?

What modes of acquisition are according to nature?

How should a father relate to his children? How should a mother? Why?

How should husband and wife relate to one another? Why?

What definition of virtue does Aristotle prefer to what other definition?

Politics II

INTRODUCTION

In Book II, Aristotle sets out to find the best regime. That regime cannot suit all people, but only those capable of living in the best way, the way that hope and prayer seeks. Consistent with the methodology he recommends in Book I, Aristotle considers features and arrangements – that is, parts or particulars – of various regimes, thereby suggesting that the best regime is not an epiphany – a whole or vision graspable all at once, but rather that elements of it are available for discovery. Hope and prayer for the ideal way of life then should spur rational inquiry.

Distinctive to Book II is inquiry into apparently model regimes: both imaginary ones proposed and existing ones praised, by a number of men – philosophers, rulers and private individuals. The philosopher Socrates, the ruler Phaleas and the urban planner Hippodamus all propose political arrangements that have never been tried, whereas the cities of Sparta, Crete and Carthage have long-established reputations.

All of these regimes however, whether they exist or not, address the problems of political unity and harmony. What unites a city and pre-empts factional conflict? All of the answers tend to focus on three matters: division of property, provisions for women and children and organization of political offices.

Aristotle pays most attention to Socrates' solutions, devoting almost half of Book II – a little over five of the twelve chapters – to discussion of Plato's *Republic* and *Laws*. Phaleas's and

Hippodamus's ideas merit one chapter each, as do the Spartan, Cretan and Carthaginian regimes. The last chapter concludes the book by considering whether 'crafting regimes' is better than 'crafting laws' or vice versa.

II. 1–6

In the first six chapters, Aristotle critiques Socrates' political proposals, as Plato presents them in his two major dialogues, *The Republic* and *The Laws*. Aristotle never mentions Plato's name, however, thereby avoiding questions that still endure about what Plato himself thought, and whether he speaks through Socrates. Evidently Aristotle does not want to discuss intricacies of the dialogues but wants rather to consider the basic features of the hypothetical regimes described therein. Hence questions concerning what Plato meant should not distract a reader of Aristotle's commentary; the issue at hand is not whether Aristotle interprets Plato correctly. Although some scholars have indeed argued that Aristotle critiques a common misinterpretation of Plato in order to expose its weaknesses, that argument would require a discussion of the ironies of Plato's dialogues unnecessary to an understanding of Aristotle.

Furthermore, Aristotle's confrontation of Socrates' arguments does not aim merely to score rhetorical points or engage in academic debate. In chapter 6 he not only compliments those arguments – 'All the discourses of Socrates are extraordinary . . . sophisticated, original, and searching' – but says in chapter 1 that they, like the theoretical designs of Phaleas and Hippodamus, usefully illuminate shortcomings of existing regimes.

Discourses of combined philosophical and practical worth begin with natural or evident questions. A search for the best regime might naturally begin then with the question, In what should citizens be partners? At the very least they should be partners in a location, but in what else? Should they go so far as Socrates proposes and share, or own communally, women, children and property? Chapters 2–5 focus on those questions by discussing the regime *The Republic* describes. While chapter 2 challenges the premise of the regime, chapters 3 and 4 criticize its arrangements for women and children, and chapter 5 considers the matter of material property, before ultimately reflecting on the regime's consequences for virtue.

According to Aristotle, Socrates presupposes an impossible end for his supposedly ideal city: namely, that it be as far as possible entirely one. To make a multitude *one* destroys its character, turning it into a household or an individual. Moreover, a city is not a multitude of similar units, like a bushel of apples or even a nation of villages. Although a city resembles a nation insofar as their respective parts provide mutual assistance, the characteristics of that assistance differ considerably, that of an alliance of villages being spontaneously responsive to contingencies and similar in kind, that of a multitude of individuals being continuous and differing in kind. The much greater interdependence of a city derives from its parts' differences. That interdependence preserves cities, since no part can survive on its own. Even when individuals are free and equal, Aristotle observes, they adopt different roles – some rule while others submit to rule – albeit each group temporarily, on a rotational schedule. Performance of reciprocal roles and functions generates self-sufficiency, the purpose of a city. Socrates' aspiration for unity thus misperceives that purpose.

In the next two chapters Aristotle criticizes both the rhetoric and the content of Socrates' proposal that women, children and property be held in common, though reserves additional criticisms about material property for chapter 5. One can interpret the phrase 'all say "mine" and "not mine"' to mean either exclusive or communal ownership. If, as seems to be the case, Socrates argues for the latter, then four negative practical consequences are foreseeable. First, neglect of women, children and things, because human beings care less for what belongs in common than for what belongs to them exclusively. Second, a psychologically unsettling state of mind, presumably more acute among fathers than mothers, caused by a system designed to prevent confirmation of suspicions, aggravated by physical resemblances, about which children are theirs. Far worse than neglect and distraction, ignorance of relatives, compared to knowledge of them, increases incidences of verbal abuse, assaults and even murder (a claim challenged by modern crime statistics). In short and third, significant conflicts are likely. Fourth and finally, so is sexual attraction between relatives and thus incest, perverting the natural affection that would otherwise bond them. All together then, the consequences of sharing women and children are as much psychological as they are behavioural; communism affects the souls as well as the conduct of human beings. It does so chiefly by weakening natural affections that spring from exclusive relationships.

Focusing on arrangements concerning material property, chapter 5 asks if possession or just use be common, or both? For example, land can be owned privately and its produce shared, or the opposite, land can be held in common and its produce divided, or both farmland and its produce can be common. But Aristotle expects complete communism as in *The Republic* to induce resentment among farmers who must provide for everyone else, such as the guardians, even though they equally own the land and are not slaves. Better Aristotle says for possessions to be held privately and voluntarily shared, which happens spontaneously among friends. Everyone still benefits and moreover things will be well cared for; as happens in Sparta, where everyone borrows each other's slaves, horses and dogs and takes what they need from nearby fields when they travel. Nonetheless, Aristotle adds, it's the responsibility of legislators and rulers to cultivate citizens who are well-disposed to one another and thus inclined to share.

Aristotle thus maintains regard for dispositions; not only do property arrangements affect the dispositions or emotions of human beings but also vice versa. A viable system of property accommodates, rather than denies or contravenes, natural human inclinations. Private ownership appeals to a person's natural self-regard or impulse for self-preservation, which differs from selfishness or greed. At the same time and paradoxically, private ownership makes possible generosity; one cannot lend or give away – for example, to friends – that which is not one's own. Even if generosity like other virtues requires or benefits from encouragement by laws and other means, its precondition is private property and its result, pleasure for the giver. Hence communism precludes generosity and therewith a very pleasurable virtue. Socrates' republic, Aristotle notes, also sacrifices another moral virtue: without monogamy men do not need to suppress their sexual urges towards various women; self-restraint is gratuitous. By robbing men of both the dignity afforded by self-control and the pleasure of giving voluntarily, communism saps them of strength and initiative.

Likewise the premise of communism, namely the common assumption that material conditions determine human conduct, fails to appreciate the complexity of human motivation. If private property causes conflict, then why do those who own property in common also fight – and in fact fight more? According to Aristotle, character more than material conditions motivate human conduct. Depravity causes disputes. Education is thus the key to societal harmony. A city should cultivate good conduct by means of families, schools and law; parents can induce habits, teachers can persuade and legislators can reward and punish acts.

Education of only the guardians and not the farmers and artisans in Socrates' republic effectively creates two cities at odds with one another. Lacking education, as well as government and laws, why would the farmers and artisans – the citizens of the regime – live peaceably and submit to the rulers? What sort of people the citizens are matters to the partnership of the guardians and the preservation of the whole regime. Complaining again about *The Republic*'s ambiguity, Aristotle questions the domestic arrangements of the ruled: if women work and are not wives but common, who will manage the household? Exacerbating the apparently radical split between the rulers and the ruled is the permanency of the membership of each: rule is not rotational. Moreover, the conditions under which the rulers live, by precluding their having any private lives at all, ensure their unhappiness. The notion that the best rulers are strictly public servants is inhumane. All together then Aristotle doubts the city's stability, longevity, harmony and happiness. How, he ultimately asks, can a whole city be happy unless most people in it are happy?

Aristotle also finds aspects of the city depicted in Plato's *Laws* problematic. Its huge military would require virtually limitless territory and moreover a guiding foreign policy. A city should defend itself as well as invade its enemies to remain formidable, but this city strangely lacks a stance on neighbouring countries. In addition, its fixed allocation of property without population control may generate widespread poverty – the surplus population would have no property, and poverty contributes to factional conflict and crime. Furthermore, while its government is practical it's not the best. A mixture of oligarchy and democracy

– that is, of rule by the few rich and rule by the many poor – it inclines more towards oligarchy, because political participation is mandatory for wealthier officials who are also more numerous and whose wealthiest hold the most powerful offices; they attend assembly and vote, and other electoral procedures are oligarchic. The government should be more mixed, more democratic. It should also be more aristocratic, paying more attention to excellence and less to wealth; and incorporate a monarchic element, leadership of an outstanding man. Overall the design of the city does not promote its goals of freedom and power. Like the city in *The Republic*, its expectations and requirements are unrealistic.

II. 7–8

In the next two chapters Aristotle addresses political proposals less radical than Socrates' sui generis idea of communism of women and children. Although put forth by men of various occupations, a good number of the proposals share the assumption that property causes all conflict. Accordingly they advance only or chiefly designs for its proper distribution, as if that were a political panacea.

Phaleas, from Chalcedon (about whom nothing else is known), advanced an equal, though privately owned, distribution. While easy to accomplish in new settlements, equality of private wealth in existing cities entails redistributive measures, such as mandating dowries only from wealthy households to poor ones, and prohibiting the latter to give them to the former. Aristotle makes two specific criticisms, each of which he quickly supplants by a general claim about human conduct. First, any effective means to equalize property must stipulate the number of offspring each household may have. But a concern far overriding relative demands on individual household wealth is the reaction of the rich, who are apt to be angered by a policy of redistribution that may make them poor. Those who maintain that property causes conflict are indeed right – when it is taken away.

Second, Phaleas's proposal for equal distribution neglects to determine the mean amount of wealth appropriate for households; people can live in equal luxury or equal penury. Superseding that oversight however is one about human desires: people may want more than an amount of property equal to that of others or, instead of more wealth, more recognition or pleasure. Although Phaleas proposes equal education along with equal property, uniformity of education does not itself temper desires: by teaching how to become wealthy, powerful or hedonistic, education may even inflame desires or ambition. Failing to see that ambition as well as need induces commission of injustices, Phaleas thinks that only satisfaction of need precludes it.

Aristotle's observation about the complexity of desires recalls his claim in his prior work, *Nicomachean Ethics*, that human beings fall into three categories: those who seek pleasure, those who seek honour and those who seek contemplation. That categorization reappears here when he adds that the sort of pleasure some seek is that unaccompanied by pains – a characterization of the activity of contemplation given in the *Nicomachean Ethics*, where he observes that all other pleasures besides thinking are preceded by some sort of physical pain, discomfort or lack: hunger before eating, fatigue before sleep, sexual urges before sex. The desire for material wealth is similarly a felt need or absence.

Accordingly Aristotle asks here, what satisfies desire for wealth, for power or recognition, and for pleasure-without-pain? He answers: for the first, a modicum of property and some sort of work; for the second, temperance; and for the third, philosophy. This second mention of philosophy in the *Politics* thus presents it as the answer to a unique and uncommon longing, that which finds no satisfaction in material things or in praise, recalling Plato's characterization of philosophic *eros*. The answer is itself a rare activity inasmuch as it does not require other human beings.

Phaleas's location of the answer to widespread discontent in property thus naïvely forgets the existence of ambitious and reflective men – a serious oversight, because it is such men who paradoxically cause the most trouble of all from frustrated desires. Whereas those who want material wealth commit relatively minor crimes, those who want power or transcendence from earthly pleasures may become tyrants or hermits – threats or burdens to a city.

The advantage of Phaleas's city is therefore not a great one. It addresses only one form or objective of desire and also fails to see its insatiability; most human beings tend to want more than they have whatever amount they have. Remarking that such people should not have authority in a regime, Aristotle indicates that the pursuit of wealth should not be a regime's ultimate objective.

In chapter 8, Aristotle turns to other ideas about what makes for a good regime, specifically those of Hippodamus, an urban planner, who designed actual plans for an ideal regime but whose personal flamboyance and lack of political experience suggests motivation by artistic ambition rather than by civic obligation. Sporting long hair, flashy robes and jewelry, he dressed moreover without regard to the season, as if concerned only with appearance not utility.

Not politically involved, his interests inclined towards natural philosophy. His apparent propensities for extremes and abstractions manifested themselves in his work: he not only invented the division of cities, but proposed a city divided into three divisions each with three subdivisions. Its population, territory and laws to be divided respectively into artisans, farmers and protectors; sacred, public and private; and cases of abuse, injury and death. Not surprisingly, Hippodamus also proposed honours for innovations benefiting the city.

Regarding these proposals Aristotle predicts, first, that farmers and artisans without weapons would become slaves of an armed militia, and second, rewards for ways to improve a regime encourage gratuitous changes as well as blackmail: alleged discovery of misconduct by officials, exposure of which would improve a regime, might be better rewarded by the officials themselves. A civic honour for whistleblowers could thereby backfire by creating more dishonourable conduct.

Other practices and institutions proposed by Hippodamus, such as election of rulers by all three parts of the citizenry and a supreme court to review appeals, do not preclude Aristotle's many queries stemming from the proposed division of the populace.

But Aristotle worries above all about the introduction of change into a regime. Change introduced into arts and sciences such as medicine and gymnastic generally improves them: new cures and exercises supplant old ones. Patients regain health more quickly and athletes and soldiers in training become stronger and faster. Extrapolation suggests the same holds for the art of politics: new laws, institutions and policies are more effective than their predecessors. Moreover, plenty of evidence indicates the inferiority of ancient laws and practices and corroborates that legislators should not preserve them for the sake of tradition but try to establish better ones. In addition, the only way to compensate for the defect inherent to law, its universality, is to change laws that result in bad outcomes in particular circumstances.

Yet if laws change frequently, then citizens stop obeying them. Imagine enrolling in a course in which the professor changes its requirements every week. You might become confused, frustrated, disorganized and resentful; refuse to meet expectations; regard him as untrustworthy; and sooner or later, fed up with its unpredictable demands, drop the course. Hence although the points in the preceding paragraph recommend out-with-the-old-in-with-the-new – that at least some laws should be changed at some times – the observation that the authority of laws depends in part on their longevity leads to a modified conclusion, namely: if only a small improvement results from changing a law, then it should not be changed, the risk to compliance not worth the benefit.

The art of politics does not then compare to other arts and sciences inasmuch as it tends not to benefit from continuous change. Preservation of laws helps preserve the regime by preserving respect for law and in turn compliance. Therefore against the advice of Hippodamus, rulers and law-makers should resist new policies promising progress. Although whatever is traditional is not necessarily good, it expects the same today as it did yesterday. Moreover, adherence to traditional ways may reflect inclinations natural or reasonable to man, further cause for leaders to think twice before abandoning them, to say nothing of the disrespect to their ancestors that abandonment of their accomplishments would demonstrate.

II. 9–12

In the last four chapters, Aristotle turns his attention to existing regimes – Sparta, Crete and Carthage in particular. He asks whether their features are suited to the best regime, and whether they are consistent with the principle of the current regime. The best regime requires leisure for its rulers, for example, so that necessary matters do not distract them, and Sparta and Crete have serfs to attend to such matters. Paradoxically however serfs' reaction to being ruled can be a distraction – the hostility of

Spartan serfs a case in point. Hence having a provision of the best regime does not guarantee that it serves a current regime; apparently such features can be integrated only with skill and judgement – the cooperation of Cretan serfs a case in point.

Similarly, the respect in which a regime treats women bears on its happiness. Spartan women live luxuriously and licentiously and dominate the regime while the men are away at war. Although the unfortunate results are not attributable to design and thus blameworthy, the mishandled circumstances manifest an inconsistency or contradiction in the regime: military discipline clashing with wanton rulers. Moreover, inheritances and dowries have given women much landed property that could otherwise be used to sustain cavalry, thereby weakening the city's defence capabilities.

Aristotle identifies other failings of Sparta, centring on its increasing democratization which, by opening more offices to the uneducated poor, enables bribery and favouritism while nonetheless appeasing the people. The characteristic hallmark of the regime, its preoccupation with war, also ill serves it, by preventing the leisure needed for thoughtful rule.

The Cretan regime resembles the Spartan because the latter imitated the former. As helots do the farming in Sparta, the subjects do it in Crete; both have common messes, but Crete manages them better by furnishing them from harvests of public land instead of asking each citizen regardless of wealth to contribute a set fee; their administrations are similar, however Crete's tendency towards dynasty generates more conflict; the isolation of Crete both protects it from foreigners and foreigners from it, and makes its subjects tolerant of rule; by contrast Sparta attacks and rules other cities and its helots tend to revolt.

Carthage appears overall to be better ruled than either Sparta or Crete. Domestically peaceful, it elects its chief council, senate and kings on the basis of desert, characteristic of the best regime. Nonetheless, deviations from the underlying principle of desert, towards democracy and oligarchy, exist. On the one hand, a sort of separation of powers operates, inasmuch as the kings and senators must comply with the wishes of the people and, on the other hand, a select committee, albeit on the basis of desert, elects its chief council and for a long tenure. Further compromising the aristocratic principle in the direction of oligarchy, Carthaginians believe that rulers should be not only virtuous but wealthy in order to have the leisure to rule well. Rulers should indeed be at leisure, but offices should not be for sale or for profit. Neither the rich nor poor should expect monetary gain from office; rather offices should furnish enough wealth to be at leisure while ruling.

Carthage's oligarchic practices would generate more conflict than they do were it not for the increasing wealth of its citizens from their foreign expeditions, allowing more to hold offices. Nonetheless, those chance circumstances do not justify the principle of oligarchy, for if they change, citizens might revolt. Better to have aristocratic laws anchored by the principle of merit.

Although many scholars doubt the authenticity of much or all of the last chapter of Book II, it makes a distinction that could be understood as key to the book: namely, that between 'crafting laws' and 'crafting regimes'. If the reader considers the entire book, the overriding arguments indicate that crafting laws – out of existing practices with a view to current circumstances – yields more viable, internally coherent regimes than does crafting regimes on the basis of policy or ideology: such as tripartite division of all features, or communism.

Chapter 12 notes that the legislators Lycurgus and Solon did both. Lycurgus crafted the Spartan regime, which has already been discussed (its chief problems – with its serfs, women and democratization – derive from its policy of imperialism). What did Solon do and how should we assess it? Although known for democratizing Athens, he is not a bringer of an entirely new order and thus a destroyer of existing modes; rather he established rule of the people by making the courts open to all. That in turn generated laws favourable to the people. Pericles instituted payment for jury duty which also, among other measures by other popular leaders, made current regimes more democratic. But again democratization was coincidental to Solon's intention. When Athens became a superior naval power during the Persian wars due to the men who devoted their service – the people, from whose ranks the men came, in turn became more demanding of power. Solon actually granted minimum power to the people, allowing them only to elect to offices from select groups and to audit officials.

The chapter ends by cataloguing a number of other legislators, and their relationships, along with a few of their contributions, exemplifying the crafting of laws rather than of regimes. For example, Philolaus contributed laws permitting adoption; Charondas, perjury trials and precise laws; while Phaleas's and Plato's proposals for crafting regimes are mentioned again, two of Plato's laws are mentioned for the first time (namely, a law concerning drinking that requires the sober to oversee drinking parties, like a designated driver, as well as a proposal that military training develop ambidexterity); both Draco and Pittacus also crafted laws, not regimes – Draco established harsh penalties, and Pittacus proposed that those who are drunk should pay a greater penalty than the sober if they commit a crime.

STUDY QUESTIONS

1. What justification does Aristotle give for analysing models of regimes that have not been put into practice?
2. Why is the end or objective that Socrates posits for his ideal regime misguided?
3. Will sharing women, and responsibility for children, work? Why or why not?
4. Should property be communal? If so, in what respect? If not, why not?
5. How do the arrangements of Socrates' city affect the exercise of liberality and moderation?
6. What does Phaleas propose and why?
7. Does Phaleas accurately perceive human desires?
8. What sort of desire does only philosophy satisfy?
9. Why does Aristotle comment on Hippodamus's personal attributes, do you suppose?
10. What is Aristotle's response to Hippodamus's proposal? List his points and summarize his conclusion.
11. Is the art of politics like the arts of medicine and physical conditioning? Why or why not?
12. Why might some traditions persist?
13. Why does Aristotle discuss Sparta, Crete and Carthage?
14. What are the consequences of Sparta's preoccupation with war?
15. Is it better to 'craft laws' or 'craft regimes'? Why? Does Aristotle's answer summarize his criticisms of the efforts of Socrates, Phaleas and Hippodamus?

Politics III

INTRODUCTION

Readers should regard the third book as crucial to a basic understanding of the *Politics*, second in importance only to the first book. It introduces Aristotle's typology of regimes, which establishes political priorities and confirms philosophical conclusions about justice initially presented in the *Nicomachean Ethics*. Specifically, Aristotle's identification and analysis of six main types of regime – kingship, aristocracy, polity, democracy, oligarchy and tyranny – demonstrate not only that three attributes are essential to a good regime – namely, wealth, freedom and virtue – but moreover, that disputes about their relative importance generate defective regimes. In other words, contrary to interpretations put forth by many scholars, Aristotle does not identify differentials in wealth or in 'class' as the root cause of political conflict, but rather the criteria of desert or conceptions of justice; men argue about the attributes that should garner political power, including but not only wealth or lack thereof. The third book also presents fundamental definitions: the definition of a city, the definition of a citizen (in chapters 1, 2 and 5) and the definition of a good man.

The general organization of the book moves from political definitions, to philosophical analysis in the middle, to political analysis informed by that philosophical analysis: thus, an ascent to a peak to a plateau. Specifically, the first four chapters conclude definitions, the fifth concerns excellence, the sixth and seventh catalogue regime types, the eighth and ninth – the middle peak – analyse principles of justice, the tenth through thirteenth discuss pros and cons of rule by the multitude and criteria of desert, and fourteen through eighteen discuss kingship. Chapter 11, on rule by the multitude, continues to generate considerable debate among scholars – some concluding that Aristotle's critique betrays an endorsement of democracy over all other regime types, others that he presents only a qualified defence that does not promote democracy over polity or aristocracy – the conclusion presented here.

III. 1

Aristotle opens Book III seeking the definition of a city. The definition is pertinent to disputes about whether a city can act;

disputes, we might note, similar to contemporary ones about whether 'society' can be held responsible for anything. On one side of the debate, Aristotle observes, are those who believe that a city does perform actions, on the other side, those who think rather that its rulers act on its behalf. In addition to rulers, however, other, non-ruling citizens inhabit a city; a city is a multitude of citizens. Clearly, then, any further definition of a city requires definition of a citizen. Thus the start of Book III – in seeming contradiction to the start of Book I – implies that the city is directed, and even defined, not by nature but by men.

Accordingly Aristotle devotes the remainder of the first chapter of Book III to the topic of citizenship. There are a number of kinds of people in a city who might seem to be citizens but are not, or are not unqualifiedly. As Aristotle says, (1) those who are given the designation honorifically; (2) foreigners, or non-natives; (3) slaves; (4) parties to contracts who are thereby subject to the law, a category that may in some places include foreigners; that is, contractual agreements do not make the parties citizens, and indeed in some places presuppose citizenship; (5) children; and (6) the elderly. It is important to define the citizen in an unqualified sense, Aristotle points out, because such a definition is necessary to resolve cases in which individuals have been deprived of civic prerogatives or exiled. He avers that citizenship is characterized chiefly by political participation: contributing to decisions in a formal capacity. That capacity may take a number of forms, including juror or member of the popular assembly. The latter are in a sense 'offices'. The term is indeed apt because those positions may have the most authority, or wield the greatest power, in a city. Nonetheless, citizenship is determined not by the *amount* of authority or power it bestows, but by its *duration*. All other political offices are of limited duration; only the 'office' of citizenship coincides with adulthood. Hence a citizen may be defined, Aristotle suggests, as one who holds 'indefinite office' in a city.

Yet, Aristotle goes on to observe, the definition is inadequate inasmuch as citizenship is necessarily, because a constituent element or conception of a regime, a function of regime type. Because regimes are qualitatively different, their respective conceptions of, or bases for, citizenship differ. Hence the above definition of citizen – one who participates throughout his adulthood in the political life of his city – may not define the citizen in all types of regimes. Indeed, Aristotle notes, that definition is suited chiefly to a citizen in a democracy; some regimes do not recognize the people as political participants, or legally mandate a standing political assembly, but rather summon groups of people ad hoc to offer their advice about cases that are ultimately decided by officials. Some regimes even assign types of cases exclusively to officials. Sparta and Carthage, for example, devote certain offices to specific types of judicial cases, such as contracts and murder, rather than turn such cases over to popular juries, as in Athens. It would appear then that if (1) citizenship is chiefly characterized by political decision-making; (2) the qualifications for citizenship vary according to regime type; and (3) regimes allocate political decision-making to certain offices – whether of definite or indefinite duration, then the definition of citizen must be revised from 'one who holds indefinite office' to 'whoever is entitled to hold a decision-making office'. (The amended definition, unlike the original one, prepares the distinction – forthcoming in particular in chapter 4 – between ruler and citizen, or ruled; only in a democracy, Aristotle has implied, are citizens simultaneously rulers throughout their adult lives.)

Aristotle concludes the first chapter of Book III by defining a city as the multitude of persons entitled to hold decision-making offices, adequate to the aim of achieving a self-sufficient life. With the second clause, Aristotle ties together the beginnings of Books I and III, and the claim that nature directs the city, with the claim that men direct it. A city cannot exist without citizens, but to constitute a city they must have the potential to achieve self-sufficiency – to fulfil themselves not simply *qua* citizens but *qua* human beings. Aristotle continues throughout the *Politics* to identify characteristics of citizens, and features of cities, which undermine that potential, as well as those that serve it, thereby indicating enduring political truths. Moreover, by defining a city in terms of the potential of citizens, Aristotle encourages citizens to keep striving while acknowledging that the end may never be realized.

III. 2

In the following chapter Aristotle raises a question related to the definition of citizenship: namely, the origin or cause of citizenship – that is, the manner in which one becomes a citizen, which means, if his above definition is invoked, how one *becomes entitled* to hold a decision-making office. There are two ways, which may be characterized, though Aristotle does not characterize them in this way, as 'naturally' and 'conventionally': namely, by birth and by law or decree. In fact the first way is commonly incorporated into and thought to be the essence of the definition of citizen: a citizen is a person whose parents are both citizens. The appeal to ancestry though eventually reveals the inadequacy of the definition by failing to account for the first citizens of a polity. By recounting a sarcastic pun attributed to a man named Gorgias, Aristotle indicates the political significance of, and potentially heated controversy surrounding, the natural definition of citizen. Gorgias said that in the town of Larisa magistrates – which is the same word in Greek as 'craftsmen' – make citizens in the way that other sorts of craftsmen make their products. If citizens are made not born, then what is to prevent making everyone a citizen? That seems to be the rhetorical question implied by Gorgias. Aristotle neither answers Gorgias directly, nor dismisses explicitly the natural legitimization of citizens. Rather, he repeats that citizenship involves the function of sharing in the regime; what determines whether or not an ancestor or a contemporary is a legitimate citizen is simply whether he is allowed to participate in political decision-making. Aristotle does not rule out the possibility that eligibility to participate may in any particular regime be determined by birth or heredity.

Aristotle then addresses the matter of citizenship by decree or rule. In doing so, he in effect reconfigures the complaint latent in Gorgias's pun: in making or creating citizens, the rulers of Larisa created them *unjustly*. Aristotle does so by describing the revolutionary change in the citizenship of Athens brought about by the rule of Cleisthenes. He overthrew a tyranny (in 510 BC) and granted citizenship to a number of foreigners and resident alien slaves. The issue raised by the example is not whether such people became citizens but whether they did so justly or unjustly. That issue raises in turn the question of whether or not a citizen correctly defined is a just citizen, which would mean that one who is not justly a citizen is not a citizen at all. Aristotle rejects that conclusion on the grounds that participation in the regime is distinguishable from the quality of that participation, as evidenced by our identification of unjust rulers.

Chapter 2 then does not simply affirm the definition of citizen arrived at in chapter 1. It shows moreover that whoever is entitled to participate in a regime may be so entitled by birth and/or so entitled unjustly. Evidently, those two ways of entitlement may or may not coincide; entitlement by birth is in practice not necessarily either just or unjust; and unjust (and just) entitlement is in practice not necessarily linked to birth. Hence Aristotle's definition of citizen, and likewise of his definition of city, is descriptive (without remaining merely empirical) rather than prescriptive.

III. 3–5

Chapter 3 returns to the subject of the city. Aristotle notes that whether citizens are so justly or unjustly relates to the earlier-mentioned dispute about whether a city can act or be held responsible for certain actions, or rather only its rulers. The outcome of that dispute is relevant to the obligations of new governments. If a democracy replaces an oligarchy or a tyranny, for example, is it obligated to fulfil agreements made by the earlier government? Some argue against, on the grounds that agreements made by unjust rulers are not legitimate because they are not to the common advantage. That would seem to be an obviously reasonable conclusion for all time, easily supported by consideration of the consequences of upholding agreements made by, for example, Caligula, the White Russians, Stalin, Hitler or Saddam Hussein. Yet Aristotle points out that the same conclusion must be drawn with respect to a democracy that is not to the common advantage: a new government would not be obligated to carry out its agreements. If it is true that only rulers and not cities are accountable, it is equally true that the people, when they are empowered, are just as accountable as the heads of governments in other regimes.

Nonetheless, the identity of a city does not appear to be reducible to its rulers. On the one hand, a city seems to be a location and all the human beings inhabiting it. In a superficial sense, Aristotle says, that is true; 'city' in common usage indicates those two physical attributes or, simply, a place. On the other hand, one location is not requisite to the existence of a city; a city may span several islands or other geographically disparate territory. If merely a unified location defined a city, then building walls around even an entire continent such as the Peloponnese would establish a city. If that were so, then Babylon would qualify as a city. Likewise, one stock of inhabitants is not requisite to a city, since a city spans many generations. The latter would suggest that the city is like a river, save that the inhabitants of a city, unlike the water in a river, can vary in character. A city is thus more like a chorus, which may be comic or tragic even while being composed of the same human beings. That is, Aristotle explains, a compound of human beings, like a compound of musical notes, can take different forms, and *the form is the key defining element of such a compound.* Neither a city's location nor its stock of people, then, is more important to its identity than its form or character, which is a function of the regime – that is, its rulers.

Thus Aristotle maintains throughout chapter 3 the theme of accountability. The identity of a city and the source of its actions lie with those who are accountable. 'Who is accountable?' is not however the same question as, 'Is their authority, and the agreements they made with it, just?'

That would suggest that the excellence of a citizen is not identical to the virtue of a good man. To confirm or disconfirm that suggestion requires examination of the virtue of a citizen – the virtue of one who is entitled to participate in decision-making – the topic of chapter 4. Citizens, Aristotle observes, are like the crew on a boat: their individual tasks differ but they share a common responsibility – namely, the preservation of their vessel, or of their regime. On one hand, then, the virtue of all citizens everywhere would seem to be the same. On the other hand, if regimes, like ships, differ in kind (e.g. some ships are for cargo, others for war), then preserving a regime, like manning a ship, will take on characteristics peculiar to its function or purpose. If that is the case, then excellence of a citizen depends on the nature of a regime and comes in many forms. If it is not a single virtue then it cannot be identical to the virtue of an excellent man.

But can circumstances bring about their convergence? For example, an excellent city? If by 'citizens' is meant all the dissimilar persons composing a city, then the answer is no – men, women and slaves have only their own particular sorts of excellence. But if 'citizen' is meant more strictly, then whether the virtue of an excellent citizen could be the same as that of an excellent man is not obvious and deserves consideration.

Aristotle begins by noting the widespread belief that the attribute that distinguishes the excellent ruler from the excellent citizen is prudence; the latter is not thought to be necessarily prudent. That is why some believe that rulers need a certain sort of education. If the good or excellent ruler and the good or excellent man are both characterized by prudence, and the good or excellent citizen is not necessarily prudent, then the virtue of the good man and that of the good citizen are not the same; or they would be the same only if the citizen is of a certain sort (namely, a good man). Further, if the citizen is one who is ruled, and happens to have the virtue characteristic of the good man and of the good ruler – namely, prudence – then he would be a man who is able both to rule and to be ruled. Hence Aristotle suggests that the rule of Jason over Thessaly (in the fourth century) was tyrannical because he did not know how to be ruled. What is praiseworthy is not simply the ability to rule, but to rule well, which apparently entails the ability to be ruled.

But being ruled is, again, the claim of a citizen; an admirable citizen is capable of being ruled well, and is also thought to have the ability to rule well. Aristotle then draws a conclusion that is puzzling because it does not follow from his preceding statements: namely, that the citizen has *more* virtue than either the ruler or the good man, if the virtue of the latter is confined to the virtue of ruling. The latter makes sense only subsequently, when he notes that ruling can mean simply mastery – that is, overseeing slaves and artisans who perform necessary work; in the case of mastery, the ruler does *not* also know how to be ruled, that is, how to perform menial labour and craftsmanship. *Servility* is not an attribute of the political ruler, the good man, or the good citizen, but rather *the capacity to be ruled as a free man.* Thus their complete virtue consists in that capacity plus the capacity to rule over free men. The moderation and justice characteristic of ruling differ according to the attributes of the ruled; men, women, children and slaves should not be ruled over in the same way. The faculty of prudence perceives differences among those who are ruled and the prudent man rules accordingly. Those who are ruled do not have or engage prudence, but rather true opinion; only in the case of the excellent citizen who is also a good man is the faculty of prudence latent, which enables him to be ruled well as a free man, without servility, until such time as he may rule over others who are free, without despotism.

Chapter 5 appears to revisit the definition of citizen. For, working from the definition arrived at earlier, Aristotle asks whether those who are not eligible to hold office should be regarded as citizens. He readily answers no, there are several categories of people who are essential to a city but should not be regarded as citizens. In particular, children, and all those adults who perform necessary services either for individuals or for the city as a whole – namely, slaves and labourers, which may include foreigners and resident aliens. Such persons should not be regarded as citizens because they are servile and thus lack the capacity to be ruled as free men and to rule over free men. That is, because they lack the potential to be good or excellent citizens, they ought not to be regarded as citizens at all.

III. 6–7

Chapter 6 introduces the question of regime types. If, as established, a regime is a governing body, and the composition of that body can vary, then regimes are of various sorts. But compositions of governments vary, Aristotle suggests, according to their aims – aims distinguishable from the aim of survival. A prevalent aim corrupts, however, the natural principle common to forms of rule hitherto mentioned: men now rule not to benefit the ruled – slaves, wives, children and their equals – as accords with nature, but to benefit themselves, in particular materially, with public funds and property. Thus Aristotle perceives a fundamental distinction among regimes: those that are unqualifiedly just and therefore correct, and those that are not and therefore deviant.

Chapter 7 identifies types of regime within those two categories by factoring in the number of rulers – one, few or many, exhausting the possibilities and revealing six types: kingship, aristocracy and polity are one, few and many ruling with a view to the common advantage and tyranny, oligarchy and democracy those respective numbers ruling with a view to their own private advantage. While the virtue of the rulers thus characterizes the first three types, the overall virtue of a multitude cannot match the overall virtue of one or a few good men; a multitude tends rather to exhibit a particular kind of virtue, namely military, which is why those men who possess arms are the most sovereign in a polity.

III. 8–9

But the two criteria, of justness and number of rulers, do not fully characterize and distinguish the six types and indeed raise, Aristotle indicates at the start of chapter 8, philosophical questions. For example, the definitions of oligarchy and of democracy: do they hinge on number of rulers or on their wealth? Circumstances muddy the definitions, for many tend to be poor and few rich. Even if the definitions combined the criteria, that would not solve the problem of what to call regimes that defy ordinary circumstances, those in which a poor minority or a well-off majority rule. The definition must then discard the accidental criterion – namely, number – that which Aristotle initially identifies as a causal differentiation of regime types. Apparently, then, the definitions of oligarchy and democracy turn out to be empirical; while Aristotle does not make explicit the reasoning that yields them, it would appear to be that, whenever the few rule in their own interest they are wealthy, and whenever the many do so they are poor. Hence he concludes that wealth and poverty differentiate oligarchy and democracy.

Once again however he disrupts that conclusion by noting in his closing remark of the chapter that everyone – whether among the rich few or the many poor, regardless of their authority in the regime – are free, meaning politically free, not enslaved or foreigners – and therefore assert claims to authority, either in defence or in pursuit of their possession of it.

Such political debate indicates deficiency from the point of view of philosophy. All fight freely over political power inasmuch as their claims challenge or defend circumstances as such, unconstrained by reason. If reasonable definitions constrain politics, then conflict between oligarchs and democrats suggest that *empirically based claims are irresolvable* and accordingly that those claims do not *define* but rather *describe* oligarchy and democracy.

That conclusion would account at any rate for the necessity of an inquiry into the defining principles of, and conceptions of justice underlying, oligarchy and democracy, which chapter 9 proposes. Common opinions about justice aren't much help because, like empirically based claims to political power, they are partial. More specifically, while people understand that justice distributes equal shares (of something), they do not recognize that the ratio between the shares should be equal to the actual – rather than their perceived – ratio between the persons; that mathematical characterization of justice, to be found in the *Nicomachean Ethics*, means that people readily agree about the relative worth of shares but not about the relative worth of individuals and that observation segues into a consideration of the relative worth of cities by indirectly raising the question of the purpose of human living. If, for example, wealth or merely being human determines individual worthiness – in other words, if the rich are better or we're all equal – then either regimes that reward the wealthy with political power and otherwise promote the retention and accretion of wealth, or those devoted solely to the equal protection of all such that no one harms anyone else, are best and politically confirm the best way of life. But if the best way of life esteems above all else, for its own sake, neither riches nor a private sphere of freedom, then neither oligarchy nor a mere social contract can be the best sort of regime.

While Aristotle does not specify here the best sort of regime, he concludes in the middle of chapter 9 that, for a city to qualify as a city, its management should pay attention to virtue. If it does not, then the partnership is merely a contract or alliance bound by law that does not make its members good and just. That remark recalls the above distinction between an incomplete and a complete conception of justice, or the distinction in *Nicomachean Ethics* V between arithmetical and proportionate justice: parties to a contract who respect one another's equal rights are insufficiently just inasmuch as they ignore – rather than recognize – one another's differences; they are legally but not duly just, right but not good.

Of course cities require legal justice and citizenship requires law-abidingness. But as Book I elaborates, cities are animated by citizens who want to live well, not merely peaceably, daily observing laws and not commit injustices against one another in order to carry out their business.

In connection with the subject of living well, the close of chapter 9 maintains the theme, upheld in Books I and II, of the importance of marriage and family. They are important not simply as institutions, but as results of affection and choice, which make life worth living. Cities cannot exist without committed households that reflect the desire and capacity of human beings to cherish and honour one another, because it is that desire and capacity that also enables proportionate justice and noble actions, the purpose of cities. Indeed, because *that*, and not merely living, is the purpose of cities, those who most foster it are more part of the city. In other words, those who are virtuous are more valuable to a city than those who are wealthy, distinguished by birth or live freely as if only living mattered. In Book I Aristotle noted the different virtues of household members and described it as a partnership requiring moral perception and considerations of justice. Thus although the penultimate line of chapter 9 suggests that those who perform just and noble actions for the city as a whole are the most worthy of citizens, Aristotle's underscoring the importance of marriage and the family just beforehand and his account of the household in Book I indicate that household members – women more than either children or slaves because of their developed reason and capacity for judgement – are also valuable members of the city. That point serves to cap then the overall argument of the chapter, that a true city is more than a compact for peace.

How that overall argument serves the chapter's initial inquiry into the defining principles of oligarchy and democracy needs to be made explicit, as does the respects in which the chapter develops, or fails to develop, chapter 8's definitions of oligarchy and democracy. While chapter 9 develops chapter 8's definition of oligarchy, from an empirical definition – a regime in which the wealthy rule – into a theoretical definition – a regime based on the claim that the wealthy *deserve* to rule because their wealth makes them the worthiest members of any polity, it does not develop chapter 8's definition of democracy in the same respect. Chapter 8's empirical definition of democracy – a regime in which the poor rule – does *not* become the theoretical definition corresponding to that of oligarchy – namely, a regime based on the claim that the poor *deserve* to rule because their *poverty* makes them the worthiest members of any polity. Chapter 9 nonetheless implies a theoretical defence of democracy. For although it makes no mention of the poor, it notes that while some claim to deserve political authority on the basis of their wealth, others do so on the basis of their *freedom*. And they extend that claim into the already noted claim or right not to be harmed by others. Thus, while chapter 9 does not even mention democracy, it implies the democratic principle of justice indicated in the *Nicomachean Ethics* as its rationale: those who are free, that is, not enslaved, should rule simply because they are free. Yet unlike elsewhere in the *Politics*, in particular in the upcoming chapter 11 of Book III, chapter 9 does not observe that the free are usually the majority and thereby ally the democratic principle to the principle of majority rule. Rather, as shown, chapter 9 indicates that the democratic principle establishes an alliance of equal individuals whose only common interest is protection from mutual harm; in other words, they value above all their own private freedom, not the economic or other interest of the majority.

Finally, by showing that an alliance for protection against harm neither reflects nor fosters the full range of human capacities, Aristotle shows it, and therewith the democratic principle of freedom or justice, along with the oligarchic principle of justice or desert, to be deficient.

That conclusion might seem to settle the question of political authority – virtuous, not simply free or wealthy, men, should have it. But the beginning of chapter 10 indicates otherwise. Allocation of authority to *any one group or man* raises problems – even rule by the virtuous, for that would deprive everyone else of the honour and privileges that political offices bestow. Yet if the poor multitude rules, they may redistribute the wealth of the few; if the few wealthy do, they may do the same to the multitude; and rule by one man may be tyrannical. Those possibilities generate at least a provisional conclusion: if such injustices result from all sorts of rule by men because of their passions, then a form of governance devoid of passion – such as law – should rule. But are not laws made by men? Aristotle asks. Indeed, if laws necessarily reflect the biased interests of those who make them, then the injustices noted above may result as much from rule by laws as from rule by men.

III. 11–13

Aristotle postpones discussion of the merits of rule by laws versus rule by men for five chapters, where he addresses it in the context of a discussion of kingship – rule by one best man. Presently, with chapter 11, he launches a systematic investigation of the still unsettled question of who should have political authority, an investigation that occupies the next eight chapters – the remainder of Book III. In light of the above scenarios, rule by the multitude – that is, democracy – might be the least problematic; at least that possibility plausibly explains why the investigation begins with it.

It is perhaps this assessment of democracy, in chapter 11 of Book III, more than any other section or remarks about democracy in the *Politics*, that has generated endless debate over the extent to which Aristotle recommends it. For while most of Book VI concerns democracy, its assessment seems, overall, less favourable than the assessment in Book III. At any rate, the two assessments together provide ample reason to debate Aristotle's view of democracy.

On the positive side, an argument for collective judgement: while no single individual among the multitude may be a good judge, or man of superior perception, all together the multitude may exercise good judgement, assuming that each individual possesses at least some virtuous attribute. Hence such a multitude is a good judge of music and poetry. Put another way, a number of people each with separate merits differs from a single man of excellence only in their lack of unity into one body. On the negative side of the assessment of democracy: the fact that not all individuals in all multitudes will be virtuous in some way, and indeed the possibility that an entire multitude may be like a herd of animals.

That downside compels the conclusion that a regime should not make everyone eligible to hold the highest offices; for with much power, defective judgement may create widespread injustices and serious mistakes. A regime should nonetheless, Aristotle adds, allow those excluded to participate in public life in some way, otherwise it will generate internal enemies, an alarming state of affairs to be avoided by those in charge. Although Aristotle does not venture the psychological dynamics, they seem easily inferable: namely, human beings want recognition and depriving them of it breeds resentment. Apparently, then, politics should heed these propensities of the human soul (or *psyche*, the basis for our word 'psychological').

To include everyone in political matters in some way, a regime could allow those not eligible for higher offices to nominate and elect those who are. That proposal itself raises a question however: can those lacking virtue or judgement recognize it in others? On the one hand, only those who have a particular kind of experience or expertise seem able to see it in others and judge its results: only a physician can assess another physician and determine if a patient is cured. On the other hand, are there not kinds of expertise that can be judged by those lacking it, and perhaps judged even better by them? For example, the arts of cooking, carpentry and, we might add to Aristotle's list, teaching: are not diners, home-dwellers and students as good or better judges of a meal, a house or a class, as other cooks, carpenters and teachers? That conclusion, combined with the earlier argument that collective judgement may equal the judgement of a single superior individual, seems to resolve the question as to whether a regime should allow the masses to choose its leaders but in fact doesn't wrestle with the central problem: are citizens good judges of leaders and leadership, as diners are of cooks and cooking? Is that an apt analogy, or are leaders and leadership rather like physicians and the art of medicine, best judged by their peers? Aristotle indicates the latter by noting the absurdity of denying the multitude authority over important matters yet granting them the right to choose those who will have such authority, as if that choice itself isn't an important matter. The only prudent electoral arrangement including the people then would restrict their power to election of office-holders to lesser offices – such as judicial court, council and assembly; not only do such positions have less power than higher ones, but they form collective bodies that serve to moderate any one office-holder's judgement.

The concluding paragraph of chapter 11 surprisingly focuses on law, recalling the end of chapter 10 which introduces the subject but then drops it by noting that poorly made or biased laws are as problematic as biased men. The focus ties in the discussion of chapter 11 however by observing that the quality of laws necessarily reflects the quality or type of the regime, and therefore deviant regimes make unjust laws. Without explicitly saying so then, Aristotle implies that the multitude should not make laws because they would make unjust ones.

So what is just? Aristotle revisits the question that he raised at the beginning of chapter 9 again at the beginning of chapter 12. Indeed, the first several lines are almost identical to those of the earlier chapter, even referencing the same passage in the *Nicomachean Ethics*. Why does Aristotle repeat himself? Perhaps the only fair inference concerns the importance and relevance of the point: common agreement that justice is equality belies widespread disagreement about the criteria of desert. Only political philosophy, he says, can ascertain the true criteria.

Accordingly he first disposes of the idea that desert or merit criteria are arbitrary. The notion that political justice may honour *any* criterion of desert, such as height, hair colour or speed, mistakenly denies that political science resembles other arts and sciences, like music and medicine, which recognize proficiency rather than irrelevant attributes. Moreover, if the criteria of justice are arbitrary then they are commensurable: any attribute or expertise could substitute for any other – wealth for height, kindness for wealth, blue eyes for kindness, scientific knowledge for blue eyes, political knowledge for scientific knowledge and vice versa in every case. Determination of the criteria of political justice therefore requires determination of human assets necessary or desirable to political community. Those assets appear to be: wealth, freedom and virtue, on the grounds that political community needs revenue and participation, and improves with good judgement. In addition to voicing their opinions, a particular sort of participation that the merely – not necessarily virtuous – free, can provide, is (bodily) defence of the regime, that is, military service. The close of chapter 12 thereby hints that a free multitude's *strongest* claim to rule, and thus the best argument for democracy, is neither their expression of opinions nor, as indicated in chapter 8, their poverty – that is, their empirical differentiation from oligarchs – but rather, their *indispensable utility for the protection of the regime*. In other words, noble service to the whole trumps both expressed opinions and demand for compensation among criteria of just desert.

Chapter 13 opens with a related paradox however. Although virtue manifested by good judgement contributes more to political justice than does wealth, free opinions or military protection, the latter are all conditions of the former. For men to rule justly, they must not be preoccupied with either survival or warfare, and thus be free to consider political matters. Paradoxically, then, the *theoretically* absolute claim to desert cannot be *politically* absolute. Indeed, because the conditional requirements of regimes are multiple, no single claim to desert or political power can be absolute in practice. If a regime were to recognize a single criterion, then it would not be an actual functional regime but merely a theoretical dystopia (perhaps like the 'city-in-speech' in Plato's *Republic*) or, at best, a short-lived dysfunctional polity.

Two observations fortify the point. First, the inseparability of, or connection between, certain virtues means that refusal of political credence to one may sacrifice another. For example, accompanying possession of wealth are virtues necessary to becoming or remaining wealthy: self-restraint, industry and upholding contracts. Similarly, those who are free – that is not deficient intellectually and temperamentally – overlap with those from healthy stock, and those of healthy stock are often the more privileged by communities and of better character. While privileges are conventional, who can say whether good character derives from nature or from nurture? One's so-called 'lineage' may involve both. Hence while political power awarded on the basis of family name alone may not be just, neither may be denial of it on the basis of family name alone.

Second, the observation in chapter 11 of the collective virtues of the majority indicates the justness of the desire of the people to rule, and thus the unjustness of an absolute claim by the few wealthy or by the few virtuous to rule.

But what if one person in a city dramatically surpasses all others in virtue? Would the same conclusions follow? That is, should he too share power with those possessing other assets important to a well-functioning regime? Aristotle answers 'no', that would be unjust, like treating a god like a mere mortal. Even if a few god-like human beings appeared, they should not share power with lesser persons either. Whether one or few, such persons are themselves law, they should not be under it. Quoting Antisthenes, Aristotle implies that only rabbit-like men believe that lion-like men should be treated the same or, better yet, ostracized – a practice common in democratically run cities and also recommended, by Periander to Thrasyboulos, to maintain tyranny.

The topic of ostracism nonetheless presents enough complexity to require more discussion, and altogether takes up more than half of chapter 13, a relatively lengthy chapter. On the one hand, a warning: by ridding cities of outstanding individuals, ostracism prevents improvement of them by way of their contributions. Without such individuals, deviant, unjust regimes may remain forever deviant and unjust, serving only the rulers, not the common good. On the other hand, a qualification: ostracism can serve the common good if it rids the city of someone characterized by an excess, except of virtue, contrary to the norm that stabilizes it, because such a man – for example, one exceptionally wealthy, large or charismatic – may dominate or sway political opinion in a way contrary to the best interests of the regime. The art of political justice, then, like the fine arts and carpentry, involves proportion.

No amount of virtue however can render justice disproportionate or destabilize a city; for virtue is judgement as to what is just and good. Hence the earlier conclusion holds: the exceptionally virtuous should not only stay in a city, but also rule – and those ruled should be grateful for their divine guidance.

III. 14–18

Chapter 14 accordingly announces a transition: the remaining five chapters of Book III will investigate kingship. The first of those five chapters describes four types and notes a fifth at the end. Although the five types of kingship differ in the sorts of domestic power they exercise, they all assume military leadership in foreign conflicts. Domestically, all, apart from the last, are law-based, which likely means limited by ancient or well-established laws which may nonetheless not prevent the king's declaration of new laws or at least of temporarily contravening decrees; that is, no description of an independent law-making body indicative of a separation of powers appears. Three of the four law-based types are hereditary, ensuring life tenure; the fourth elective and the fifth unspecified as to manner of replacement. Moderate scope of authority characterizes two of the four law-based types – the Spartan model and the feudal benefactor model; whereas barbaric tyranny and elective dictatorship exert more authority. Stability nonetheless characterizes the latter two because the citizens do not resist rule; their willing submission derives in the first case from their non-Greek dispositions and in the second case from their voluntary choice of leader. The fifth type of kingship mentioned exercises complete authority, like the head of a household.

Kingship as such is good, but is complete authority? The question becomes, then, whether rule by the best man or by the best laws is better. Laws are defective because of their universal not circumstantial application, yet advantageous because dispassionate. Rule calls for attention both to circumstances and law. The question now becomes, should one man or many rule along with law? Many are more incorruptible by passion, but there's no guarantee that the judgement of many will be reasonable and not undermine law. Supposing however a reasonable majority, their rule would be preferable to that of one reasonable man, because of the latter's greater vulnerability to passion; hence the superiority of aristocracy to kingship – by all evidence, a decisive verdict.

Unfortunately past aristocracies have deteriorated, into oligarchies and then tyrannies due to embezzlement by progressively fewer hands, and then into democracies, as a result of reaction to tyrants and growth of cities. Aristotle does not say here how that deterioration might have been prevented but notes in subsequent books that rulers should not be able to profit from their office and cities should not be unduly large.

Rule by one best man has merits, but what if a king rules according to his own will? Among persons who are equal, that would be unjust; only rule by turns would be just. Rule by law should nonetheless complement rule by men because, insofar as it renders *a priori* the same verdict to similar situations, it is more impartial – invulnerable to spontaneous spite or favouritism. Customs are even better than both rule by laws and rule by men, evidently because they combine the discretion of rule by men over time and impartiality. Both law and custom however derive from the judgement of many men and therefore should guide the judgement of actual rulers, who should be several in number rather than one because they are apt to be more dispassionate.

Kingship and polity are preferable to rule by several virtuous men – aristocracy – only if, in the first case, the populace is disposed to be ruled by one greatly surpassing them in virtue and only if, in the second case, a multitude possesses military aptitude and concedes rule to the well off. The final verdict of Book III thus declares aristocracy to be the best of the six types of regime.

STUDY QUESTIONS

1. What is the definition of a citizen?
2. What defines, or constitutes the identity of, a city?
3. What defines a ruler?
4. Do the virtue of citizen and that of the ruler ever intersect?
5. Is a good citizen necessarily a good human being, and vice versa?
6. For the sake of what do human beings establish cities?
7. What makes regimes 'correct'? What makes them 'errant'?
8. How many types of regimes are there? Why? What are they?
9. What generally defines the types of regime? What is the specific defining principle of each regime type?
10. What 'must be a care for every city'? Why? Is that matter a care (or concern) of liberal democracies today? Should it be?
11. Aristotle denies that the city is what sort of entity? Why?
12. Do the respective empirical definitions of oligarchy and democracy correspond with their respective defining principles of justice?
13. What is Aristotle's view of rule by the multitude? Does he identify any merits of it? Any shortcomings? Do his observations pertain to any institutional or governmental practices in present-day liberal democracies?
14. What is the best justification for democracy?
15. Does every good quality deserve political recognition?
16. Does any one quality deserve exclusive political recognition, or recognition above all others? If so, what is it and why does it deserve that recognition? If not, why not?
17. Should a regime ever ostracize individuals? Why or why not?
18. What is the foremost advantage of kingship, common to the five types described in chapter 14?
19. Should laws or men rule? Is either decidedly superior? Why or why not?
20. What is the best of the six types of regime? Why?

Politics IV

INTRODUCTION

In Book IV, Aristotle discusses regime types with an eye to the best possible regime. His approach suggests that practiced correctly, political science can offer a comprehensive and useful commentary because it aims to understand regimes as they are intending their improvement. In this spirit, Aristotle builds upon his early discussion of regimes by focusing on the two most common forms of government, democracy and oligarchy.

While regimes come in all shapes and sizes as political opinions vary, the most obvious fact of political life is that one cannot be wealthy and poor at the same time. It is what individuals make of this defining feature of cities that helps shape them along partisan lines. The best oligarchic and democratic regimes consider the merits of wealth and its democratic corollary, freedom, and establish 'mixed' governments as circumstances allow.

Aristotle develops this argument in Book IV. He sets out in chapters 1–3 to explain what prevents political observers from understanding regimes correctly, hinting that most partisans lack the requisite philosophic disposition. In chapters 4–6, Aristotle provides working definitions for democracy and oligarchy and describes varieties of each. Introducing tyranny, polity and aristocracy into the discussion, he further highlights the differences between better and worse forms of democracy and oligarchy in chapters 7–13. Chapters 14–16 deal with the role that political institutions play in shaping regimes. In sum, Book IV provides a particularly useful account of how the dispositional state of various oligarchies and democracies provides excellent clues as to what helps preserve and destroy all regimes.

IV. 1–2

Aristotle announces a four-part agenda at the beginning of Book IV; specifically, to consider (1) the best regime simply; (2) the best regime for a particular city; (3) the best way to preserve a given city, and (4) the best possible city. Postponing his discussion of the best way to preserve a given city until Book V, Aristotle introduces the first, second and fourth parts of the discussion by relating the study of regime types to the study of athletic training.

Aristotle models his study of political science on athletic training because it is both a comprehensive and practical science. As the athletic trainer takes into account the connection between physical regimens and the material circumstance of human bodies, the political scientist ought to do the same when considering forms of governments and cities. Such an approach prompts one not only to ask what is best simply, but what is best for each, and what is best for all in common. Additionally, while the untrained eye is drawn into making unrealistic judgements about what is best, better and the best possible in the realm of politics, athletics provides a sober reminder of the practical constraints involving human affairs. The knowledgeable athletic trainer presupposes that there is an ideal regimen for the ideal physical specimen yet also takes into account that most men are not ideal physical specimens. In other words, it is difficult when imagining the ideal athlete, say Michael Phelps, to ignore the reality that while we are not Phelps, we could very well benefit from a type of athletic training that aspires to this ideal yet fits our particular circumstance or is accessible and beneficial to all.

Aristotle contends that other commentators on politics, in failing to take up the subject of regimes correctly, have produced interpretations that are less useful. Some have focused purely on the best regime at the expense of the attainable whereas others have been inattentive to existing regimes because of their attraction to a single regime (e.g. the Spartan). Aristotle's improved approach, which provides an understanding of the different types of regimes, how regimes can be combined, and how regimes necessitate distinct laws, offers a framework through which all regimes can be viewed properly, and perhaps improved.

This explains in part why in relisting the three 'correct' regimes – kingship, aristocracy and polity – and their corresponding deviations – tyranny, oligarchy and democracy – Aristotle treats polity with the three deviations in the discussion to follow. In Book III, Aristotle distinguished 'correct' from 'deviating' regimes based upon whether or not the authoritative element within it ruled with a view to the common or private advantage. Aristotle grouped the polity, the rule of the many who serve for the advantage of all, with kingship and aristocracy. In listing the polity with the regimes in need of improvement – democracy, oligarchy and tyranny – Aristotle reiterates his earlier suggestion that it is difficult for the many to rule with an eye to virtue while at the same time laying the ground work for his argument that the polity is the best possible regime for most.

Along the same lines, in discussing which of the three deviations – tyranny, oligarchy and democracy – is worst, he defines democracy as the most moderate of the three. Indirectly referencing Plato, who identified regimes as being 'better' than one another based upon the standards of efficiency and lawfulness in the *Statesman*, Aristotle suggests that regimes instead should be considered as 'less bad' to the degree that each approximates virtue, insofar as the good of the largest number, even if not all, is sought. Whereas Plato criticizes democratic regimes as incapable of greatness, either good or bad, and remains open to the prospect that the one or the few could rule lawfully, Aristotle's partitioning of the discussion between 'best' and 'best possible' reduces the practical discussion of regime types to four, and places the polity as the 'best possible' of the four. Aristotle's partial buttressing of the rule of the many stands quietly yet importantly in the background in Books IV and V as Aristotle takes up the subject of the varieties of oligarchies and democracies with an eye to what is attainable and choice-worthy.

IV. 3

After re-cataloguing the main regime types in his introduction so as to emphasize the practical nature of the discussion to follow, Aristotle considers why the main regime types vary. His simple answer is that regime types vary because the 'parts' of the city vary. Cities are composed of households, some rich, some poor and some of the middling sort. In turn, rich and poor households practice different occupations and are either armed or unarmed. And while the city is also differentiated into parts based upon the role played by family and virtue, Aristotle – in keeping with the theme of how the untrained eye views politics – initially defines wealth as the predominant factor that divides the city.

Aristotle's account of why regimes vary is somewhat different than his earlier treatment of the subject at the beginning of Book III. There Aristotle also suggested that the city is made up of parts, before moving promptly to a discussion of that part of the city – in the person of the citizen – that is entitled to rule. In both

Books III and IV, regimes differ because the arrangement of offices differs in each city. But whereas his focus in Book III is the identity of the citizen per se, in Book IV Aristotle is most interested in the circumstances that dictate one arrangement over another. The distribution of power and equal status dictate different circumstances in each city. Some parts are more preeminent than others; some parts are 'more equal' than others. A city's disposition accurately reflects how various parts within it view their relative status.

While Aristotle's philosophic disposition allows him to differentiate between regimes based upon the character of the ruling element within it, most people differentiate regimes by counting the number of rulers. Because the clearest divide within the city is brought on by the disparity in wealth, most observers conclude that there are two sorts of regimes, oligarchy (the rule of the *few* who are wealthy) and democracy (the rule of *many* who are not wealthy). History is filled with political commentaries, struggles and campaigns guided by this partially true yet disproportionately emphasized approach. Recognizing that most view politics this way, Aristotle accentuates his coverage of democracy and oligarchy. By providing a more enriching discussion of democracy and oligarchy – one that trains the popular eye to do more than count – his commentary prepares readers to take a more comprehensive view of regimes, and to consider how the varieties of each may be improved.

IV. 4–6

Aristotle begins his tutorial on democracy and oligarchy by explaining why people mistake democracy as simply the rule of the multitude and oligarchy as simply the rule of the few. He introduces two seemingly impossible scenarios to prove this point; namely, that it would be inaccurate to describe the rule of the many wealthy over the few poor as democratic or the rule of a superior poor few over the many wealthy as oligarchic. A democracy is properly characterized when all free persons have authority and, likewise, an oligarchy when the wealthy hold power.

Yet Aristotle is not completely satisfied with an improved definition of democracy and oligarchy that emphasizes quality over quantity because regimes, made up of multiple parts, are defined by many qualities. In particular, three historical examples necessitate a more precise definition of democracy and oligarchy. First, what are we to make of regimes, like the Egyptian, which distribute offices to the few not on the basis of wealth but on the basis of physical stature? As it would be improper to define the Egyptian regime as oligarchic, this example shows that superlatives other than wealth are used to differentiate and grant status to the few. A second difficulty is encountered in the Apollonian and Therean cases, two cities in which the few free rule over the majority who are not free. Aristotle suggests that freedom is not always the defining attribute of the many. He introduces a final complexity in the example of the Colophonians, a city made up of a majority of wealthy citizens prior to their war with the Lydians. The example of the Colophonians shows that majorities are affluent in extraordinary circumstances.

Aristotle settles on a more precise definition of democracy, the rule of the free *and poor* majority, and oligarchy, the rule of the wealthy *and better born* few, by showing once again that proper judgement on the subject of regimes requires the possession of an investigative disposition to see beyond simple categorizations of rule based merely upon number.

Aristotle also introduces the role that occupational activity plays in differentiating democracies from one another. Democracies differ because their populations, like the populations of all cities, engage in farming, the necessary arts, commerce, labour and war to varying degrees. Here he invites a comparison between his own city and Socrates' 'happy city' or 'city of pigs' in the *Republic*. At least two important differences between the cities stand out. First, Socrates' city lacks a military element as originally instituted. Though Socrates later adds this necessary element to his city, Aristotle suggests that he does not do so soon enough. Yet the more significant correction Aristotle makes is to include, as Socrates does not, an adjudicative/deliberative element in his list of the city's principal occupations. Socrates eventually discusses the role played by reason in the person of the philosopher-king in ordering the city's affairs aright. Aristotle insists in his presentation that the establishment of the regime – as it represents the body politic's arrangement of offices – is a primary, necessary and determining element within the city from the start.

Perhaps this explains why Aristotle compares the city with an animal, positing that both are made up of different parts that provide for its necessary needs. Aristotle's mention of animals and human beings in the context of cities prompts his audience to think back to his earlier definition of the city. In Book I, chapter 2, Aristotle posits that human beings, unlike other animals, are constituted so as to judge, deliberate and perform other political functions. As the 'political' part of the human being is more of a part its constitution than its body, the 'political' part of the city should take precedence over parts relating to its necessary needs.

Political judgement requires that one understand which regime – or arrangement of offices – is just. A select group within the city need not perform this role, as people are capable of simultaneously carrying out multiple tasks within the city, and therefore should not be constrained by a definition of justice such as the *Republic's* one man/one art. While wealth allows some to perform certain public service and magisterial duties, less affluent individuals can perform most deliberative and adjudicative functions. A capacity for political virtue, rather than the accumulation of wealth, is the key to the just performance of these tasks.

Here a summary is helpful. The *Politics*, and in particular Aristotle's discussion of regime types, serves as a preparation for understanding which regime is just. In displaying the disposition required to understand and improve regimes (comparing the political scientist to the practical and comprehensive athletic trainer), producing a more accurate definition of the two most common regimes (democracy and oligarchy), and clarifying what functions may and may not be performed by the many and the few, Aristotle enables rulers to overcome common misperceptions about politics. Since democracy and oligarchy are the most common regimes, and democratic and oligarchic rulers are prone to make judgements on a quantitative rather than a qualitative basis, Aristotle's discussion is essential to partisans of either of these two regimes. Oligarchs and democrats understand that it is impossible in both empirical and theoretical terms for the same person to be poor and wealthy. Aristotle's analysis of the types of democracy and oligarchy in chapters 4, 5 and 6 suggests that it is what they make of this truth that greatly influences the degree to which these regimes are ordered correctly.

Laws that treat rich and poor as equals characterize the 'first' sort of democracy where freedom serves as both an ennobling and enabling force. The greatest temptation facing democratic partisans is to punish the wealthy for their affluence by limiting their opportunity to participate in the regime. In this 'first' type of democracy, liberality – in terms of the overcoming of petty prejudice for the sake of allowing reasonable access to office-holding – spurs right judgement. Aristotle writes more about what conditions would enable such a democracy to come into being later in Book IV yet he provides a preliminary answer as to why such a regime may be as uncommon as it is praiseworthy in his further ranking of democracies.

The second, third and fourth types of democracy share with the first an insistence upon standards for participation in the regime. Aristotle teaches, however, that the standards of wealth, birth and citizenship do not provide perfect appraisals of human worth. How much of a wealth assessment is too little or too much? Are birth and citizenship excellent criteria for judging who should rule? The democratic use of such criteria makes the regime more accessible to the common man yet also demeans the office itself. In short, of what value is office-holding if every-one can be an office-holder?

Another consequence of using loose qualifications in arrang-ing offices is the adverse effect it has on the authority of the law. Because little respect is given to office-holders, laws become less authoritative. As office-holding becomes a pedestrian affair, the multitude begins to question the entire legitimacy of the regime.

Good sight enables individuals within the 'first' type of democ-racy to judge that equality in one respect does not equate with equality in all respects. But as categorization of human equality becomes generalized, good sight and judgement give way along with respect for office-holding and the law. The democratic citi-zen goes from being an active participant in the regime to being an inactive part of a whole. While granted nominal authority, democratic citizens in more extreme democracies soon are com-pelled to hand over power to popular leaders who flatter the multitude and soon discard the democratic form of government altogether.

Aristotle's description of the worst type of democracy is similar to Plato's account of democratic vices in the *Republic*. Both political philosophers show that democratic regimes suffer when passion for freedom and equality runs amuck. However

Aristotle allows for the possibility that democracy need not collapse into tyranny. When assisted by a more thoughtful regard for both office-holding and the law, democratic regimes are better able to harness their citizens' love for freedom and equality. Aristotle goes so far as to reason that democracy of the tyrannical sort is not, in fact, a regime. For if the laws do not rule, and particular judgements are not made by office-holders, the regime becomes an entity that loses all sense of justice and thus the title of regime itself.

A second difference between Aristotle and Plato's presentation is that Aristotle shows that a comparable scenario might arise in oligarchies when the few make too much of qualities that are relatively less important. As the discussion turns to oligarchy, Aristotle demonstrates that intellectual corruption that leads to tyranny is not a democratic problem per se, but a problem that troubles all regimes.

In the first type of oligarchy, an assessment is required of all office-holders, yet is low enough to enable many to participate in the rule of the city. Higher assessments define the second type of oligarchy. Aristotle suggests that such large assessments could be considered aristocratic if inclusive of all offices and oligarchic if limited to special offices. As was the case with the more unreasonable forms of democracy, a third type of oligarchy uses a birth requirement to delineate prospective office-holders. Rather than encouraging participation, oligarchic assessment and birth requirements limit the participation of the multitude.

The more discriminating oligarchic approach to selecting office-holders in part guards the regime against the city's worst elements. Yet Aristotle shows that taken to the extreme in the fourth type of oligarchy, a 'dynastic' regime, selectivity-turned-nepotism tends towards tyranny because oligarchs incorrectly assume that inequality of wealth justifies inequality in all regards in spite of merit. In other words, extreme deference to status (in terms of wealth) is as blinding to the oligarch as is egalitarianism is to the democrat.

Aristotle spends the remainder of chapter 5 defining a mixed democratic/oligarchic regime (an idea he also considers at the beginning of chapter 6) and introducing the topic of how time and revolution make regime analysis even more complex (which also previews his critique of Plato's examination of regime change that comes at the conclusion of Book V). Aristotle notes that there is a type of regime in which the laws are not popular yet the regime is governed in a popular fashion because of the character and upbringing of citizens. Likewise, circumstance allows for popular laws and an oligarchic citizenry. Aristotle teaches that crosscurrents within regimes enable oligarchic and democratic elements to co-exist. But just because advocates of more pure forms of democracy or oligarchy are willing to wait out change does not guarantee that the regime will remain mixed for long.

Only when Aristotle gives us a more complete understanding of why democracies and oligarchies change in chapter 6 do we encounter a regime whose laws and rulers operate in the true spirit of a mixed regime. The regime that promotes the most sincere mixture of democracy and oligarchy is that which appropriates features of both, a regime in which most are engaged in farming, have a moderate amount of property, and rely upon the law to help rule the regime. Self-governing out of necessity, it is not their extensive participation in office-holding that makes them support the regime more than it is their realization that the law shields it against excess.

However most democratic and oligarchic regimes tend away from the mixed regime model. For example, the first type of democracy uses an assessment that acts not so much to constrain more than to conflate the necessary ingredients to good governance. The regime is coarsened as a result as individuals are judged worthy of office not so much based upon wealth as their ability to take advantage of the small assessment to use their free time to rule. An allowance for all of unquestioned descent and all free men to rule in the second and third types of democracy further signals that leisure perhaps has enabled too many to govern. Describing the fourth and final type of democracy, Aristotle argues that abundance enables all, rather than the pre-eminent, to share in the arrangement of offices. Paradoxically, broad affluence encourages a political environment in which wealth is held in low regard. The many poor use their new-found comfort and influence to disregard both democratic office-holders and democratic laws.

A similar corruption plagues oligarchic regimes. The first kind of oligarchy possesses a large middle class. Many in this regime own a moderate amount of property, busy themselves tending to their wealth, and submit to the rule of law. When fewer oligarchs possess greater fortunes, their desire for further aggrandizement clouds their political judgement. In this regime, human pre-eminence, in the form of wealth, supplants a clear and recognized law. Although the last form of oligarchy still provides for the arrangement of offices, its dynastic features make it more like its tyrannical democratic counterpart than the other oligarchic types.

IV. 7–13

In the chapters that follow, Aristotle's presentation of aristocracy and polity (and tyranny) serves not so much to provide an understanding of these less common regimes as it does to expand his discussion of oligarchy and democracy. Aristotle begins by noting that oligarchy and democracy are often confused for aristocracy and polity, respectively. People regularly equate good birth, reputation and respectability with virtue. Similarly, polities are mistaken for democracies because they are so rarely established.

Aristotle's definition of aristocracy as the rule of the virtuous recalls his earlier discussion in Book III, chapter 4, where he described the good man, the good citizen, and the good ruler. At that time, he posited that good men, possessing prudence, knew how to rule as well as be ruled. In the best regime, all those who are eligible to rule, that is, all citizens, are good men. Thus, only in the aristocratic regime is the good citizen also a good man. Conversely, good citizens in democracies, oligarchies and the like are good in terms of their relation to the regime. The good democratic citizen is assessed on the standard of freedom and the oligarchic citizen is assessed on the standard of wealth.

As stated above, aristocracies are most commonly mischaracterized as the rule of the rich. Because some are elected to office on the basis of wealth, desert, reputation or respectability, men fail to differentiate these attributes from virtue. Men also mistake aristocratic rule as the rule of the wealthy because they assume that the affluent are gentle, dignified or worthy. Less frequently, aristocracy is confused with compound aristocratic/democratic and aristocratic/constitutional aristocratic forms as these regimes concern themselves with virtue in addition to people and/or wealth. Aristotle's final catalogue of aristocracies includes the best regime, and its oligarchic, democratic and constitutional variants.

As people mistake aristocracies for oligarchies, they also fail to tell polity and democracy apart because the defining principle of polities is the mixing of elements. In chapters 8–9 and 11–12, Aristotle offers two definitions of polity that involve the blending of parts. The first definition, offered in chapter 9, understands the polity as a combination of oligarchy and democracy. This mixture is produced in one of three ways: through melding democratic and oligarchic arrangements, through finding a mean between the democratic and oligarchic arrangements or by taking some from both the oligarchic and the democratic arrangements. Aristotle posits that we know a good polity when we don't see it; that is, when its parts are so well blended as to make it difficult to define the regime as either democratic or oligarchic. Perhaps this explains why Aristotle uses polity generically. The regime that is difficult to make out is easily construed as the body politic itself. Aristotle gives the example of the Spartans as a type of regime that finely mixes its democratic (educational and communal institutions) and oligarchic (electoral and political institutions) elements.

Aristotle also defines polity as the rule of the middle class or middling part in chapter 11, revisiting his description of the city as composed of three parts – wealthy, poor and the middle class. A large homogeneous middle class provides a different, yet equally effective safeguard against democratic and oligarchic radicalism. Both this and the earlier types of mixed regimes share a common regard for the preservation of the regime. The Spartans best exemplified this spirit, as none – regardless of status – desired a change in regime. In the mixed city, political partnership is strengthened by uniformity as a contented middle-class neither plots against the wealthy nor disenfranchises the poor.

It is curious that Aristotle takes up the subject of tyranny in the context of celebrating the moderation of the mixed regime. He excuses the break by suggesting that he simply means to be comprehensive while noting that there is not much debate about the subject specifically. He compares tyranny with kingship and notes that there are two types of tyranny that, in an important way, overlap with monarchy. As barbarians choose plenipotentiary monarchs, the ancient Greeks often chose dictators to lead them. These tyrannies are worthy of the name 'regime' because they are based upon law and consent even if the regime operates according to the tyrant's will. A third type of tyranny stands in stark contrast with the first two types as the tyrant rules over the unwilling for his own advantage. Aristotle suggests that even among tyrannies, an important distinction must be made between rule over the willing and the unwilling.

Aristotle's account of the third type of tyranny also serves to highlight the polity's most important attribute. While the polity is not afforded the advantages of the various types of equipment that might make the city virtuous, it best prevents the excesses of wealth or freedom from creating lawlessness, division and faction within the city. For political partnership to come into being and to be maintained among citizens, citizens need to believe that all are engaged in a common cause. The reality that extreme democrats and extreme oligarchs so easily mistreat their fellow citizens reminds the reader of the worst form of tyranny, and explains why such regimes left unchallenged could either vanquish their own in times of faction, or destroy others in their ideological attempt to remake foreign cities in their own image.

Are men predominantly moderate or extreme? Aristotle intimates in naming the middling regime or polity as the best possible regime that while men should not expect true aristocracy to come into being, they should rule in a manner that best encourages a strong middle-class, broad participation, and laws designed to procure such an arrangement indefinitely. Most regimes are either democratic or oligarchic because the middling part is often small, and powerful partisans seek pre-eminence at a cost to the city. If men could be more reasonable, and recognize that each part of the city desires recognition, perhaps things would be different. But most men do not want to live according to a just arrangement and instead seek power or desire to make their disempowerment palatable. Hence given the disposition of most men and most cities, Aristotle does not leave off discussion of the best possible city on an encouraging note.

Aristotle does, however, propose a means to encourage moderation in chapter 12. As cities are composed of quality and quantity, maintaining a lasting regime involves persuading the quantitative element of the city to respect notions of quality and persuading the qualitative element of the city to respect notions of quantity. Legislators encourage such blending when they promote the middling part of the regime to the fore. For those in the middle not only help forge a common political identity, but also act as the surest counterweight to partisanship that threatens the survival of the city. Aristotle also shows in chapter 13 how offices might be arranged so as to maintain the mixed regime. Most importantly, regimes should be designed so as to encourage each part to have a stake in the city's preservation.

IV. 14–16

Aristotle completes Book IV by discussing how deliberative, official and adjudicative political institutions differ from one another. As has been Aristotle's habit throughout his discussion of regime types, democracy and oligarchy receive special attention.

Chapter 14 discusses the role that deliberative political institutions play in the operation of a regime. The deliberative part of the regime considers war and peace, alliances and judgement and auditing of public officials. As for the democratic or popular way of deliberating, the mode in which individuals take turns deciding matters influences these institutions. Officials can take turns, decide together, decide together on some matters and allow officers to administer all other affairs or meet to deliberate and decide on all matters (the operational mode of the final form of democracy, dynastic oligarchies and tyrannical monarchy). Likewise, oligarchic deliberation is similarly divided between different modes, with the few taking on a larger or smaller role based upon how oligarchic the regime is. Central to Aristotle's coverage of the mode of deliberation is his advocacy of a middling approach in which the few and the multitude share power. When necessary, fines, offices defined by jurisdiction, and electoral practices should be used to encourage the participation of the people as well as the wealthy.

In chapter 15, Aristotle lists the ways in which officials are selected. He begins by identifying the true office-holder as the individual who is in command or superintendence over a part of the city's affairs. Aristotle writes that as some officers are more necessary than others, other questions (such as centralized or decentralized administration and the degree to which regimes influence the types of offices present within the city) influence officialdom. Every city must account for the amount of manpower on hand and the kind of manpower available when deciding upon what offices are necessary.

Aristotle again prescribes mixing oligarchic and popular power when considering who selects officials, from whom officials are selected, and in what manner they are selected (by election or lot). The most democratic system of selection is for all to select from all by election or lot. The most aristocratic system is for some to select from all, or all from some, by election. It is interesting to observe that modern liberal governments employ a more aristocratic method of selection because their principle is choice of the best rather than random choice. Perhaps in part this helps to explain the relative stability of modern liberal democratic regimes.

In chapter 16, Aristotle takes up the adjudicative office, once again describing the various methods regimes use when selecting judges and granting them jurisdiction over different matters. Noting that different courts have jurisdiction over different arenas of public life, he argues that the most important courts are the political courts because they have jurisdiction over modes of selection or participation within the regime. As mixing oligarchic and democratic elements is necessary for the proper functioning of the city, adjudicative matters that influence the political make-up of the regime must be considered as an essential part of the political equation.

CONCLUSION

In dealing with the practical difficulties and opportunities present within all regimes, yet particularly those common to democracy and oligarchy, Aristotle accomplishes what he sets out to do at the beginning of Book IV. The best regime is clearly aristocratic. While all cities should aspire to aristocracy, cities must make do with what they have. The best possible regime for most cities – the regime that is most fitting for most – is polity, a mixed regime. Because most cities are democratic or oligarchic, this teaching above all aims to sets the record straight for democrats and oligarchs. Improved democratic and oligarchic statecraft requires an understanding that partisans will always make arguments for arranging offices on the grounds of wealth and freedom. When rulers rightly understand the role partisanship plays in the affairs of the city, they can best counteract elements that lead to the regime's dissolution. Good laws and good demographics are required for such a regime to come into being. But only stable, moderate and reasonable rulers and citizens can keep such a polity in existence for long.

Taken together with his coverage of politics in Books I–III, Aristotle shows in Book IV that there are no strictly theoretical solutions to political problems. One can encourage democrats and oligarchs to be more reasonable, but the best possible solution is to make practical improvements to each regime. A regime that is torn apart by the few wealthy who have no regard for freedom, or the free and poor multitude who have no regard for wealth will become lawless or collapse altogether under the stresses of faction. As shown in chapters 14–16, the best safeguard against these undesirable alternatives is to arrange offices prudently. Thus while Aristotle's discussion in these closing chapters reads as somewhat less exciting than his analysis of the influence of human disposition on regime types, his practical advice is of primary importance to the proper functioning of existing regimes. The lure of ideology will always complicate political matters for oligarchs, democrats and political scientists. Yet Aristotle makes available to his audience a comprehensive and accessible means to political improvement.

STUDY QUESTIONS

1. What is Aristotle's stated mission or agenda in this book? What in particular does he want to determine in connection with the subject of regime types?
2. Why do even the main types of regime vary?
3. How does Aristotle define 'regime' in Book IV, chapter 3? Recall his definition of a city in Book III.
4. Although many sorts of regimes exist, they are commonly identified as one of two types; into what two types does common opinion group regimes? Why?
5. What traits characterize democracy? Why?
6. What is the chief reason that democracies differ from one another?
7. What 'must be regarded as more a part of cities than things relating to necessary needs'?
8. What quality does that part require?

9. What characterizes 'the first sort' of democracy? Why, do you suppose, Aristotle calls it 'the first sort'?

10. Democracy wherein 'the laws are without authority' – that is, lawless democracy – resembles what other type of regime? Why? (In Plato's *Republic*, what type of regime does democracy degenerate into? Why?)

11. What is 'a reasonable criticism' of democracy of the above sort? Why?

12. What is an oligarchy comparable to the above sort of democracy called?

13. What characterizes 'the first kind of oligarchy'?

14. What according to Aristotle is the precise definition of aristocracy? Does the definition recall his earlier discussion, in Book III, chapter 4, about the good man, the good citizen and the good ruler? According to that earlier discussion and the definition of aristocracy, what must be true in an aristocracy?

15. What is the more common definition of aristocracy?

16. In Book IV, chapters 8–9 and 11–12, Aristotle mentions 'polity'. What is 'polity'? Is more than one definition given? If so, what are they? Is there one defining principle, or theoretical definition of polity? Why or why not?

17. According to Aristotle, what regime 'is best for most cities and most human beings'? To what kind of regime does he contrast that regime at the beginning of Book IV, chapter 11?

18. Is the regime discussed in Book IV, chapters 11–12, one of the six main types of regime, a seventh type, or a type at all? Defend your answer.

19. What are the characteristics of the regime discussed in Book IV, chapters 11–12?

20. According to chapters 13–15, who should be encouraged to participate in what types of regimes, why, and by what means should they be encouraged?

21. According to chapter 15, what considerations determine, in the case of each regime, which sort and how many offices are necessary, and what sort are not necessary but rather useful to achieve an excellent regime?

22. What is the most democratic system of selection? The most aristocratic system? Is one system more commonly used by liberal governments today?

23. Of the three kinds of courts identified in chapter 16 – those concerning criminal matters, those concerning foreigners and 'political ones' – the latter are most important. When the matters over which they have jurisdiction are not well handled, factional conflicts and even revolution can result. Why?

24. By the end of Book IV, has Aristotle determined what he set out to determine at the beginning of the book? If so, what is that determination? If not, why not?

25. Does Book IV (in combination with Book III) provide instruction or guidance to rulers? If so, how would you summarize that instruction or guidance? If not, then why not?

Politics V

INTRODUCTION

Aristotle carries the theme of mixture from Book IV into Book V, where he discusses the third question stated at the beginning of Book IV (as apparently part of that book's agenda); namely, what type of government preserves a city in less than ideal circumstances? Aristotle's answer is that the most secure form of government does not stimulate factional conflict by ignoring the desire of different sorts of citizens for a voice in government. No government should become so extreme that it grants political offices or privileges only on the basis of free birth or of wealth; extreme governments breed resentment and that resentment may mobilize citizens to change the fundamental structure of the regime. In short, preservation requires moderation.

Aristotle's lesson that regimes sometimes revolve or metabolize into different sorts altogether is particularly valuable for democratic and oligarchic audiences. If a regime is oligarchic, it should incorporate ways to include the poor in some political decisions or otherwise give them privileges or benefits (e.g. the practice of jury duty began in ancient Greece as a way to include the people in the affairs of a city). Likewise, if a regime is democratic, it should not alienate the wealthy by redistributing wealth nor entirely exclude them from governance.

Aristotle continues his call for political moderation in Book V by first considering revolution and factional conflict in general terms in chapters 1–4 before examining the manner in which these phenomena appear in specific regime types. As has been his habit throughout the *Politics*, he pays particular attention to regime change as it takes place within democracy and oligarchy. Aristotle's coverage of the topic includes an investigation into how aristocracies, polities, monarchies and tyrannies are destroyed and preserved. Perhaps foreshadowing his critique of Socrates' account of regime change in Plato's *Republic*, he is intent to show that regimes need not spiral downward unidirectionally, but that in fact, enlightened statecraft, to the degree it is possible within any regime type, might improve political conditions within any city and thus prevent its collapse. Aristotle therefore pays special attention to what attributes might allow statesmen within various regimes to preserve their cities in chapters 7–9.

A final preliminary note on Book V: the modern reader may be taken aback in reading through Aristotle's discussion of the preservation of kingships and tyrannies in chapters 10–11. Aristotle offers advice to tyrants on how they might maintain their rule over cities without insisting that they become more virtuous. Given that his discussion of tyranny overlaps with his presentation of the more inferior forms of democracy and oligarchy, perhaps it is enough for Aristotle to show leaders in these regimes that it is in their best interest to treat all of their subjects with at least a modicum of dignity. Thus while vicious democracies, oligarchies and tyrannies might not become virtuous, they at least might become less vicious. Read in connection with Socrates' discussion of the corruption of human character as cities devolve from what is best to what is worst, Aristotle leaves open the possibility that political science might temper the worse forms of political rule.

V. 1

Aristotle's starting point for discussing the destruction and preservation of regimes is his finding that while all agree to some definition of justice based upon equality, democrats and oligarchs in particular mistake equality or inequality in part for equality or inequality simply. Thus wrong judgement fans the flames of partisan discontent between democrats and oligarchs. Presumably, factional conflict between these parties is seldom, if ever, just.

Conversely, factional conflict would be justified if those who are outstanding in virtue challenged the regime. Yet aristocrats lack in revolutionary desire what they merit in standing as virtuous citizens. Valuable because their disposition enables them to understand the limits of politics, aristocrats are least likely to participate in factional conflict. They most effectively participate in politics by persuading others to become more moderate. If this sounds like Aristotle's objective in writing the *Politics*, the reader is on the right track.

Factional conflict may or may not change one regime into another. When factional conflict changes a regime into an altogether different regime, the result is a 'revolution' or 'constitutional transformation'. Instances of revolution include transformations from democracy into oligarchy and vice-versa, or from either of these regimes into a polity or aristocracy or from aristocracy into a polity. Other times factional conflict produces partial changes as fomenters seek only to fortify or dilute a regime type, change part of it, or shift power into different hands.

Inequality is the cause of factional conflict. Democrats view equality in numerical terms, unhappy if men are treated unequal to one another regardless of any significant differences. Oligarchs view equality in proportionate terms, angered when men of distinction in part are treated as equals in any significant regard. Because nearly all men measure each other using qualitative or quantitative criteria, and these notions of worth often contradict each other, the most common regimes, oligarchy and democracy, are often in opposition. Aristotle's partial solution to oligarchic/democratic tension is to encourage men to incorporate quantity and quality as standards of worth to the extent that either regime favours either measure to too great a degree.

This helps explain why Aristotle includes the positive transformations of oligarchy and democracy into polity or aristocracy in his cataloguing of these types of factional conflict. Aristotle's list of possible factional conflicts does not include a political transformation from polities to aristocracies. Conceivably the mixing of regimes into polities represents the extent to which this type of improvement can be achieved through factional conflict. In other words, the virtuous stop short of making partisan demands for the best regime given their recognition of the limits of politics.

Also important in Aristotle's initial discussion of how conflict arises in particular regimes is his remark that non-factional or

privately motivated change occurs most typically within oligarchies and monarchies. Aristotle suggests that personal interest
plays a particularly keen role in movements within these regimes.
In fact, Aristotle closes chapter 1 by indicating that all things
being equal, oligarchy is more prone to factional conflict than
democracy because it is challenged both from within (when oligarchs fight with one another) and from without (when popular
forces rise up against the few). Rarely do democrats rise up
against the regime, leaving democratic forms of government
with only oligarchic revolution to fear. Consistent with Aristotle's outlook to this point, the most stable regime is the regime
that combines democratic and oligarchic elements in a manner
that satisfies the few and the many or diminishes the differences
between them.

V. 2–4

Aristotle outlines the causes of factional conflict and revolution
by emphasizing (a) the condition of men when they engage in
factional conflict, (b) their rationale for doing so and (c) the
signs that factional conflict is about to occur. Having described
fomenters of faction as advocates of particular definitions of
equality, Aristotle notes that men also challenge regimes for
profit and honour or to avoid loss and dishonour. Additionally,
arrogance, fear, the desire for pre-eminence, contempt, disproportionate growth, electioneering, underestimation, neglect of
small things and dissimilarity cause factional conflict. While the
primary and underlying cause of revolution and factional conflict relates to the disposition of the body politic, Aristotle spells
out how disproportionate growth, gradual alteration, dissimilarity and territorial division facilitate political transformation.

Revolution sometimes occurs when one part of the city
becomes quantitatively or qualitatively disproportionate to the
other parts. At times, leaders simply ignore their city's changing
composition. Sometimes, disproportion is dictated by events.
Aristotle mentions the decline of the Athenian nobility resulting
from Sparta's successful land campaign as an example of the
type of revolution produced by circumstance.

Change is also generated, albeit more gradually, through the
modification of election laws. Foreshadowing his later discussion of the role of deceit in attempting revolutions, Aristotle

hints that institutional change is no less significant than spontaneous change as small adjustments over time add up to substantial transformations altogether.

Dissimilarity also plays a role in factional conflict and revolution, as cities are predisposed to divide along racial and/or
cultural lines. Aristotle cites numerous examples of the role that
tribal identity plays in making or breaking political associations.

Cities also are prone to fracture along territorial lines. Aristotle once again cites the example of the Athenians in showing that
those who lived within the Piraeus (the Athenian port) were
more popularly inclined than those who lived in Athens proper.
Even the smallest territorial differences can create important
political divides.

Aristotle's point with regard to the manner in which revolutions occur is to show that revolution and factional conflict are
neither overly complicated nor simple phenomena. One can
comprehend in part the causes of revolution and factional conflict because both scenarios involve human activity predicated
by desire and/or circumstance. Yet the rise of revolution and
factional conflict is not perfectly intelligible because men are
multifaceted beings who seek change for manifold reasons.

The unifying element of all explanations of revolution and
factional conflict is that men use their sight, often times incorrectly, to judge both themselves and others. Individual, proportional, institutional, racial, cultural and territorial differences
are categorized by sight. Note that Aristotle posits at the end of
chapter 3 that perhaps the greatest factional split is between virtue and depravity. This factional split is not, however, played out
in a violent partisan struggle more than it helps to explain why
men have so much difficulty moving beyond partisan struggle.
Without a virtuous disposition that enables one to understand
men as they are, individuals instead cling to categorizations that
make political distinctions easy, and thus both palatable and
prone to volatility.

Perhaps the greatest impediment to preventing factional conflict and/or revolution is that human beings have a difficult time
recognizing these phenomena when they are most easily assuaged.
Aristotle uses three examples to demonstrate this point. In referencing a love affair that leads to a factional split, Aristotle recommends that special oversight should be given to the affairs of

the prominent and powerful as their private affairs often ignite passions within the public sphere. But how would it be possible to know when the seemingly harmless affairs of less prominent citizens might create problems in the public square? Here Aristotle references the story of two nameless brothers whose quarrel over an inheritance leads to partisan warfare between popular and affluent elements in Hestiaea. Can every quarrel between brothers be prevented before the fact or toned down after it begins? And even if the affairs of brothers could be accounted for, can the same be said of unforeseen events such as the example of the bridegroom who left behind his bride at Delphi because of a bad omen? Are there not instances where men quarrel over matters that cannot be decided one way or another? One need only walk into the legal proceedings of familial disputes throughout the world to understand how easily such affairs both spiral downward and spill over to the public square to the detriment of private parties and political communities alike.

Aristotle notes that oligarchic and democratic partisans are apt to use private disputes to facilitate faction. While it is unrealistic to expect that each and every private dispute could be recognized and defused, the most secure regimes are ordered in such a way as to prevent private quarrels from becoming public catastrophes. Such safeguards are best instituted during the organization of regimes as once faction appears; the more reasonable elements within the polis tend to give way to those with manifest strength.

Aristotle completes his introduction to factional conflicts and revolutions by noting that regime change is attempted and secured through the use of force or deceit. Making no judgement as to which method is better or worse, he curiously mentions the case of the Athenian contingent (led by Alcibiades, the infamous student of Socrates and alleged Athenian traitor) near the time of the collapse of Athens' democracy as an example of revolutionaries who used deceit to procure and force to secure change. If the best measure of a regime's value is its approximation of virtue, are the means used to effect regime change less fundamental than the actualization of that scenario which is best? Also noteworthy is that Aristotle makes no mention of the use of honest persuasion to effect regime change. Moving forward in Aristotle's coverage of regime change, it is important to keep in mind to what degree he thinks men are educable in this regard.

V. 5–7

In Chapters 5 though 7, Aristotle particularizes his examination of regime change, focusing his study on whether or not (a) some regime types are more prone to change than others, (b) particular problems arise in particular regimes, and (c) specific safeguards tend to counteract the dangers of revolution and factional conflict within particular regimes.

Aristotle begins by exploring revolution within democratic regimes, asserting that present-day revolutions within democracies occur when the affluent revolt against the many poor who have become overtly hostile to their interests. In these scenarios, the multitude, led by aspiring demagogues, harass the wealthy by redistributing wealth within the city.

Revolutions with democracies once took place very differently. Popular leaders in older democracies – which were much smaller – were less skilled in rhetoric than in war. The multitude, busy at work, granted power to military types who in turn used their strength to tighten their grip upon the regime. Gaining the confidence of the multitude because of their seeming antagonism to the wealthy, popular leaders of old were entrusted to protect the interest of the many. Democracy evolved into tyranny when these popular leaders began to rule for their own advantage.

In more contemporary settings, however, popular leaders are skilled at rhetoric rather than war. By inflaming the people's passions, they threaten its well-being by stirring up oligarchic opposition. Perhaps their shortcomings in waging war explain why popular forces, once aroused, tend to be overcome by more militarily-prepared oligarchic reactionaries.

Given these developments, Aristotle posits that the best means to secure modern democratic regimes is to institute election reform. If elections take place at the local level, and are thus more tribal in nature, demagogues will have less opportunity to stir up the multitude. In effect, by making democratic regimes more localized on the basis of tribal representation rather than what today we would call direct democracy, Aristotle limits the ability of modern popular leaders to use their rhetorical flair to cast demagogic spells on the multitude.

Aristotle's prescription for securing democratic regimes is interesting given his introduction to regime change in chapters 1–4. Aristotle's earlier argument was that most revolutions and factional conflicts take place because private disputes spill over into public affairs. But the problem with revolutions in democracies in Aristotle's day is not so much that they spring from private affairs but that unruly multitudes are readymade political puppets for rhetorically gifted demagogues.

It is intriguing that half of Aristotle's references to the city of Athens in the *Politics* occur within his presentation of revolution. Overwhelmingly Aristotle's mention of Athens corresponds to difficulties it faced during the Peloponnesian War, when, for a time, it became an oligarchy. Might Aristotle be suggesting that Athens is the contemporary democratic regime writ large, most powerful when it attained international prominence, yet also more prone to destruction due to the unmanageable nature of democratic politics on such a grand scale? In Athens' instance, however, the Spartan-led collection of primarily oligarchic city-states brought an end to its political hegemony rather than any domestic oligarchic uprising. Given the context of Aristotle's discussion of force and fraud, Athens presents a particularly interesting case study, as some of its most prominent democratic leaders during the Peloponnesian War were as unskilled militarily as they were rhetorically.

Democracies thus break apart when the oversized and impersonal nature of politics directs the regime further away from the rule of law, encouraging the many who are free to become an unmanageable multitude. Oligarchies, on the other hand, suffer from a different fate as those within the regime engage in unhealthy rivalry. In essence, oligarchy is threatened more by factional conflict than it is by revolution. Perhaps this is explained because there is that much more power, or money or honour to be had within the regime itself. The resulting private squabbles create scenarios where the rule of the affluent few becomes the rule of the hated elite. Aristotle's portrayal of revolution within oligarchies reads a lot like his earlier description of the phenomenon at the beginning of Book V in which internal rivalry between private parties turns into factional dispute between larger groups within society. It is in these instances when popular parties are brought in to fight for competing groups of oligarchs, or when oligarchs elect to lead popular revolts that revolutions occur.

Oligarchies remain most secure when all of the few are satisfied. In other words, if no one has too much power, or too much honour or too much wealth, oligarchs can live peaceably with one another. Affluence tempered and tended to helps ensure a stable environment through which oligarchies can be preserved. Hence as democracy is made more secure by preventing the many from becoming a mob oligarchy is made more secure by ensuring relative parity among a critical mass of oligarchs.

Aristotle also discusses revolution in the case of aristocracy and polity. Unlike his depiction of revolution within democracy and oligarchy, Aristotle does not place complete blame upon aristocrats for their own undoing. Instead, aristocracies suffer revolution because insurgents are unable to distinguish between prominence based upon the possession of virtue and prominence based upon the possession of wealth. To the degree that aristocratic revolution is set off by the misjudgement of its rulers, the greatest trouble is caused when slight deviations change the regime over time. This explains why aristocratic revolutions often occur unnoticed. Over a period of time, political compromises that are forced upon aristocrats by the few and the many lead to their downfall.

Note that Aristotle references the Peloponnesian War once again at the close of this discussion, remarking that regimes are sometimes overturned from inside and sometimes from outside. As the study of revolution and factional conflict must account for external developments, the example of the Athenians and the Spartans in the Peloponnesian War shows that in addition to collapsing from internal causes, democracies and oligarchies can also be destroyed when each abandons itself in the hope of crushing its foreign, and seemingly opposite, regime antagonist. Had the more aristocratic types within both the Athenian (Pericles) and Spartan (Archidamus) regimes held more sway throughout the war, they might have been able to protect their regimes from collapse. Unrestrained, both the Athenians and the Spartans come to practice progressively inferior forms of democracy and oligarchy as the war proceeds.

V. 8–9

As things can be destroyed they can also be preserved. Aristotle's general rule for leaders is to provide in opposites that which threatens the regime's survival. For example, if lawlessness threatens a regime, rulers should attempt to reinvigorate the rule of law. If small things unnoticed produce big things, it is important for rulers to keep track of embryonic developments with an eye to longer term consequences. Such careful observation of small things, however, should not lapse into pettiness and small-mindedness as the ruler should attend to small and great matters to the degree they merit attention. Aristotle suggests that a leader's ability to understand the relationship between parts and wholes is a key ingredient to understanding politics in real time.

Aristotle provides specific examples of how such a disposition might benefit political communities. With regard to effective rule within oligarchies, it is important that rulers treat equals equally. If one merits reward, it should not matter who one is. A proper respect for equality is the most effective antidote to the oligarchic tendency to disenfranchise the many or to engage in dangerous rivalry with the few. Most importantly, oligarchs should guard against individuals growing powerful or acquiring prominence too quickly. In other words, it is the amount and speed with which one acquires power that often determines the extent of one's corruption. The best cure for this oligarchic disease is to establish a system in which men are rewarded based upon what they merit rather than based upon their political connections.

Continuing a theme that runs through Books IV and V, Aristotle posits that rulers should mix opposing parts within the city and/or increase the power of those who make up the middling part of a body politic. This can be accomplished, in part, by making it difficult for men to profit when holding office. If all have the opportunity to serve, yet little can be gained for oneself through public service, the poor will spend their time at work and the well-off will be less able to steal from fellow members of their communities.

Aristotle also recommends instituting penalties for oligarchic rulers who treat the multitude arrogantly. Furthermore, he calls for an effort to ensure that wealth is not siphoned into the hands of the few. In sum, all of Aristotle's prescriptions aim at shaping oligarchies so as to secure the allegiance of a critical mass of the few and the many. If the affluent scorn the many or the many molest the wealthy to the point of creating faction, the regime will soon collapse under the weight of the city's unhealthy disposition.

Because revolution is best thwarted by wise statecraft, it follows naturally that Aristotle directs his discussion to the attributes of good rulers. It is paramount that rulers have affection for the regime, the capacity to rule, and a virtuous and just character. Aristotle observes that some offices require more of one attribute than another. For example, positions that require specific skill sets, such as generalship, should not be given to well-meaning dolts. Because effective generalship is rare, the office should be filled by one who might fall short on some fronts, but has the military wherewithal to lead fighting men to victory. Conversely, individuals who possess all three qualities should perform less distinctive roles.

Aristotle's examination of good rule brings up an interesting quandary. Most citizens at least outwardly desire leaders who are effective, patriotic and virtuous. But what about instances when effectiveness might require a leader to eschew virtue or vice versa? It would seem that in the best scenario, a leader would possess and act in accordance with all three attributes. But if a regime's survival is its overriding concern, the best possible ruler is the one who keeps the regime intact by sustaining it as the most viable alternative for his fellow citizens. In other words, of what good is ruling or virtue if one lacks a regime?

Yet Aristotle also argues that regimes are like noses in the sense that the straightest nose is the best, but given that most noses tend to approximate the standard, it is second best that they not be further mangled by artists who represent them. Aristotle contends that while compelled to work with the regime that is given to them, rulers can practice politics in a manner that makes what is naturally imperfect better or worse. Affection and skill count but rulers with virtuous dispositions are best able to rise above partisan or utopian zeal that prompts them to attempt either the uncharitable or the impossible, respectively. The best possible ruler, like the best possible artist, in working with what he has, contributes to the development of a thing so as to bring forth the fullest measure of beauty it can attain. From this vantage point, one's possession of justice or virtue would appear to be paramount.

So one should neither cut off one's nose to save one's face or contort a nose in a manner that renders it dysfunctional. In both cases, it appears that excellent statecraft necessitates a moderate disposition. The best statesmen not only realize that extremism in one direction or another is unhealthy but also understand that differing political forms needn't be discordant. In real terms, the best democratic and oligarchic leaders see to it not only that their preferred political form is preserved but also that opposite elements within the city are incorporated into the regime. Such foresight is enabled by their uncommon recognition both of the limits of their own conceptions of justice and the extent to which their political opponents raise legitimate political concerns. When ideology trumps good sense, regimes are worsened as a result. Ideally, democratic and oligarchic rulers would possess a liberal persuasion that engendered regard within their political communities for the good and dangerous elements within both conceptions of justice.

It is paramount that leaders place a high priority upon the education of the citizenry. For as cities consist of laws, leaders and habits, it is excellent to have just laws and great leaders, but if the excellence of the regime does not extend to the character of its citizenry, they in turn have the ability to corrupt both laws and leaders. What then does it mean to be educated? Are good democrats or oligarchs educated well simply by being converted into partisan democrats or partisan oligarchs? No. The best democratic and oligarchic leaders excel because of their liberality and the depth and breadth through which they understand other parts or elements within the city. Educated citizenries should, to the degree it is possible, mirror such leaders.

Those oligarchies and democracies that are believed to be especially oligarchic or democratic are not the best oligarchies or democracies because instead of defining oligarchic or democratic forms of justice rightly, extreme definitions coarsen the character of the citizenry. The overdone oligarch lives a life of luxury that in turn produces his own indolence and the resentment of the multitude. Likewise, the overdone democrat lives the life of unrestrained freedom and equality that in turn produces lawlessness and the opportunity for oligarchic reaction or the rise of tyranny.

V. 10–11

Aristotle concludes his discussion of revolution and individual regime types in examining the preservation and destruction of monarchical regimes. Aristotle begins by noting that kingship and tyranny are different in that a king is a monarch who rules over a willing people, whereas a tyrant rules over unwilling people.

Kingships correspond to aristocratic regimes because kings, pre-eminent in virtue – whether as a result of their high calibre as individuals, benefactors or men of good birth, are most deserving of rule. In ideal circumstances, beneficent kings guard against the excesses of the people and the affluent in their relations with one another.

Tyrannies, on the other hand, correspond to the most depraved or deviant forms of democracy and oligarchy. Tyrants come into being as cities grow, kings become corrupted or oligarchs aggregate power. The pleasure-seeking tyrant creates a regime that looks like himself by eliminating the pre-eminent and creating faction among the citizenry. This explains Aristotle's mention of Periander's advice to the tyrant Thrasyboulus to lop off all the pre-eminent ears of corn. Periander's counsel, quite simply, was that tyrants best consolidate power by making all equally depraved.

It follows that kingships and tyrannies face different threats to their survival. Given that kings rule over willing populations, only dramatic changes in the disposition of the populace endanger their rule. Kings must be careful not to anger citizens by treating them arrogantly or by appropriating their property. A king must remain magnanimous as Aristotle's coverage suggests that even those who once ruled well over a willing population can become corrupted. Perhaps the greatest problem kings face is that their even-handed administration of public affairs encourages those with a combination of courage and skill to attempt their undoing. It appears from Aristotle's presentation that liberality sometimes invites mutiny. Aristotle notes that seldom is regicide committed for greed or profit. Rather what commonly motivates insurgents is their desire for recognition or praise.

Conversely, tyrannies are often destroyed by external powers. For as the good king procures the respect and allegiance from a willing people, the undisciplined tyrant inspires hate and contempt among his populace which leads them to seek help from abroad. Much as people hate tyrants because of the pain they exact on political communities, they are contemptuous of tyrants because of their extravagant living.

It is thus easy to see that kingship is Aristotle's favoured form of monarchy. But kingships seldom arise because men of high calibre are wanting, and even when available, people are rarely willing voluntarily to pay homage to such men.

If tyranny is thus the more prevalent form of monarchy, Aristotle's best hope for political reform is to convince the tyrant to become more kingly or to inspire those yet to be ruled by onerous tyrants to be on the lookout for signs of their impending rise. What the people (both the few and the many) lack in foresight, the tyrant lacks in virtue. By showing the populace how to spot a bad tyrant or by teaching the bad tyrant to be less vicious, Aristotle enhances the possibility that tyranny might be refined.

In eliminating the pre-eminent, preventing people from associating, keeping men ignorant and busy, overseeing the affairs of men and engaging in wars, tyrants both neuter and preoccupy those within a political community who might challenge their rule while at the same time elevating politically the worst elements within society. The tyrant's goal is to decrease the number of respectable persons in his realm. By making men feeble, cowardly and distrustful of one another, the tyrant obstructs gainful citizenship that might later threaten his hold on society. For a time, the tyrant's efforts work. Yet Aristotle later notes that bad tyrants, no matter how effectively they carry out such efforts, have short life expectancies.

Aristotle submits that the best way for tyrants to secure their power is not to turn men into depraved slaves, but to become more kingly. The kingly tyrant, while acknowledging that he had once ruled over an unwilling mass, should attempt to increase the number of willing participants in his rule. Once again, Aristotle notes that the key to a regime's survival (even tyrannies) is the presence of an agreeable citizenry. As mentioned earlier, inferior forms of tyranny, oligarchy and democracy are the most vulnerable of all regimes because they are held together by the will of obsessed rulers rather than by the law, the presence of office holders, and an educated citizenry. As tyrants become more dignified, avoid arrogance, drunkenness, licentiousness and so on, and conform to the part of kings, they increase the likelihood that those around them will find them deserving of rule. In essence, Aristotle here advises tyrants to use their power to create authentic regimes.

Tyrants can also secure their power by preventing men, and especially the bold, from becoming great, and by reforming the regime gradually. The tyrant must work to discard all reminders of his former oppression as he introduces a new mode or order of doing things. Furthermore, concerning his relationship with the few and the many, the reformed tyrant should seek to encourage the rise of moderate elements within the regime as Aristotle has recommended throughout his presentation. Perhaps in doing so, the tyrant keeps the political community satisfied and thus best guards against the type of spiritedness that would lead to an attempt on his life. It is critical to note that Aristotle leaves open the very real prospect that such a political transformation need not involve a tyrant's personal renewal. For as shown in his reference to Theopompus, it is better to hand over longer lasting, if weaker, monarchies to one's descendants if such a plan of secession makes more certain one's own political survival.

V. 12

A possible key to Book V appears in its final chapter. There Aristotle criticizes Socrates' account of revolution in Plato's *Republic*, which presents regime change as both inevitable and cyclical.

In taking up Aristotle's commentary, it is helpful to begin briefly with a summary of Socrates' account of revolution in Plato's *Republic*. Socrates' search for justice at the beginning of the *Republic* leads him, with the aid of his interlocutors, to create a 'city in speech'. Ideally, Socrates asserts, this city would be ruled by philosopher-kings, who in establishing a city dedicated to justice, would best enable men to live good lives. The great problem, however, of anything created by, of, and for human beings is that it is bound to decay. The decay of Socrates' ideal city is brought on by its leaders' failure to defend the city against faction once deficient men come into power. Much of the remainder of the *Republic* characterizes the ideal city's devolution into timocracy (the rule of the spirited), oligarchy (the rule of the wealthy), democracy (the rule of the free and equal) and tyranny (the rule of the powerful). Socrates' suggestion is that all things political tend from better to worse.

While Aristotle doesn't disagree with Socrates that some persons are born inferior – that is, incapable of being educated, and are thus the source of political degeneration, Aristotle points out that such individuals contrast not only with excellent men, constitutive of the best regime, but also with men constituting lesser types of regime (as if to suggest that there are degrees of educability). Aristotle further points out that if uneducable individuals are born into an aristocracy, then the regime would degenerate even more radically than Socrates claims: not only into timocracy but into its 'opposite sort' – by which he may mean here democracy, rule by the uneducated or vulgar.

Another problem with Socrates' portrait of revolution is that it assumes that revolution occurs simultaneously within all parts of the city, carrying away everything in its path. But as Aristotle makes clear throughout Book V, change occurs on many levels, and often involves the presence of cross-currents that blunt if not impede the progress of revolution. The city, as constituted of many parts, can have dispositional tendencies in many directions at once. Therefore to argue as Socrates does, that aristocracy monolithically changes into timocracy, is to overstate the city's homogeneity.

Aristotle also observes, that 'revolution may also go the other way': regimes may improve, not just degenerate. Aristotle thereby implies, as his foregoing analysis indicates, that men, in their capacity as citizens, rulers and legislators, can effect change for the better as well as for the worse. The prospect that regimes may improve as well as degenerate compels the reader to note Aristotle's earlier suggestion that even tyrannical regimes might be improved. And although Aristotle does not explicitly say so, if regime change is cyclical as Socrates implies, to assume that the worst type of regime might regenerate into the best as the cycle begins anew would be reckless given the character of the worst forms of tyranny, democracy and oligarchy.

Neither time itself, nor alleged historical forces, necessarily overpower human initiative. Contrary not only to the apparent allegation of Socrates, but also to modern theories of revolution put forth by Hegel and Marx, regime change is neither inevitable nor unidirectional. Aristotle's criticism of Socrates therefore directs the reader back to the analysis he provides throughout chapter 5. Understanding that revolution is natural to human communities, political science is concerned with understanding how leaders might secure regimes against change for the worse and improve their regimes so as to procure change for the better.

STUDY QUESTIONS

1. What is the general cause of factional conflict?
2. Who 'would engage in factional conflict most justifiably, yet they do it the least of all'?
3. What is 'revolution'? How is it related to factional conflict?
4. Which is more stable and freer from factional conflict, oligarchy or democracy? Why?
5. For the sake of what do men engage in factional conflict?
6. What are some early signs and causes of factional conflict?
7. In what manner do revolutions occur?
8. Are multiracial and multicultural populations more or less likely than racially and culturally homogeneous populations to split into factions?
9. At what point in the development of factions should rulers be most concerned?
10. From what 'small things' can factions develop?
11. What can power shifts in a regime result in?
12. Why usually do democracies undergo revolution?
13. What are the most common causes of revolution in oligarchies?
14. What are the most common causes of revolution in aristocracies?
15. What are the most common causes of revolution in polities?
16. Why are revolutions in aristocracies more apt to be overlooked than in other types of regime?
17. What can rulers do to help their regime last?
18. What qualities should those who hold office have? Do citizens everywhere (or do you) look for such qualities in their (your) leaders? Should they?
19. How is a regime like a nose?
20. What contributes most of all to a regime's longevity?
21. What would it mean to be educated relative to a regime type? Why?

22. Are democracies that are believed to be especially democratic, the best democracies?
23. What did Periander advise Thrasyboulus to do? Does Aristotle think this is good political advice? Why or why not?
24. What are the most common causes of revolution in monarchies?
25. What less commonly motivates an attack against a monarch?
26. What are the main reasons tyrannies are attacked?
27. What do extreme oligarchies, extreme democracies and tyrannies have in common?
28. Why do kingships 'no longer arise' according to Aristotle?
29. What kinds of kingships are more lasting?
30. Why does Aristotle discuss the ways in which tyrannies are preserved?
31. How are tyrannies made more lasting?
32. Which regime types are the most short-lived? Why?
33. How do revolutions proceed according to Socrates? Does Aristotle agree?
34. How would you summarize Aristotle's analysis of revolution? Is it like or unlike other analyses or theories of revolution that you know of? In what respects?
35. How would you summarize Aristotle's advice about regime change? Can certain kinds of change be prevented, and other kinds encouraged?

Politics VI

INTRODUCTION

In Book VI, Aristotle examines freedom and orderliness, the defining principles of democracy and oligarchy, respectively. Building upon his critique of Socrates' account of revolution in the *Republic* at the end of Book V, Aristotle first gives greater definition to freedom as a political principle in chapters 1–5, suggesting that democracy need not collapse into tyranny because of disorder bred by license. In chapters 6–8, Aristotle likewise shows that oligarchies might be ordered so as to secure the regime without disenfranchising major elements within the city. In sum, Aristotle concludes that rightly understood and encouraged, freedom and orderliness contribute to the proper maintenance of regimes and cities.

VI. 1

Aristotle notes that variety within regimes and the existence of 'aggregate' and 'compound' regimes greatly influences how forms of government are preserved and destroyed. Aristotle once again indicates that revolution is neither uniform nor unidirectional because cities consist of composites of human types, and these composites change over time.

Of great importance to Aristotle given the attention he pays to oligarchy and democracy throughout the *Politics* is Socrates' argument that both regimes ultimately transform into tyranny. Conceivably, Aristotle continues his coverage of revolution, paying particular attention to democracy and oligarchy, because of the compelling nature of Socrates' indictment of these regimes. Hence much as Socrates must overcome the claim that justice is the advantage of the stronger at the beginning of the *Republic* in order to proceed with his investigation into the nature of justice, Socrates' account of revolution forces Aristotle to offer an alternative explanation of regime change, especially as it comes to pass within democratic and oligarchic cities. Aristotle's objective in Book VI is to describe democratic and oligarchic revolution without making light of that which draws both regimes towards tyranny. Aristotle accomplishes this task by showing how democratic and oligarchic governments are drawn away from freedom and orderliness, the two principles that encourage the proper functioning of each regime, respectively.

VI. 2–3

Aristotle first sets out to define popular rule. He argues that there is not a single kind of democracy because different mixtures of people produce dissimilar democratic cities. Understanding the varied nature of regimes enables rulers within any regime to better comprehend how their regimes might best be improved or preserved. The greatest obstacle to democratic improvement and preservation is the tendency among most democrats to aggregate everything related to democratic governance under the heading of freedom. Rightly understood and instituted, freedom signals the complete sharing of rule among all. Democrats incorrectly assume that only democratic governance can create the political conditions in which freedom is established and/or extended.

Likewise they mistakenly assume that it is impossible for men to enjoy political freedom in other regimes.

Setting out to explain why democrats make these errors, Aristotle suggests that freedom is best understood by its markings. The best way to determine whether a city is free is to ascertain if its regime defines justice in terms of freedom and encourages its citizens to be free. In the freest city, men are ruled and rule in return.

Because democracy involves the rule of the many, and the many justify their rule based upon their numbers, they incorrectly assume that nowhere more do men experience freedom than in such a setting. In other words, zealous democrats believe freedom is the defining principle of democracy because they equate the rule of the many with the actualization of freedom.

Aristotle, however, maintains that participation in the regime as defined by majority rule does not necessarily translate into the equals ruling and being ruled in return. The many often rule in a manner that is antithetical to freedom. Just because democrats think democratic governance leads to the spread of freedom does not make it so, and often times their misunderstanding on this point endangers the political principle they claim to care most about. Many centuries later, Abraham Lincoln would use a similar line of reasoning in rejecting his political opponent Stephen Douglas's fashionable claim that the success of the American experiment in self-government depended upon the extension of popular sovereignty. Lincoln recognized that left unconstrained, a majority of Americans could very easily deny to one another the natural rights upon which the American regime gained its fullest expression.

A second mark of freedom is viewed by considering whether or not men live as they want. Aristotle calls this mark the 'work of freedom'. Proponents of freedom often mistake allowing people to live as they want for the notion that everything must be permitted. Aristotle maintains that the mode in which men enjoy freedom helps signify whether or not they are actually free. Simply doing what one wants does not equate with freedom. Often times, such a definition of freedom translates into harming or disenfranchising others, especially those with less standing. Aristotle argues that freedom is better characterized when men have an equal opportunity to do what they want, regardless of their status.

Aristotle devises a means in which political freedom might be realized in a divided city. His system, mathematical in nature, calls for accounting for definitions of justice offered by both the few and the many. While the few contend that decisions should be made on the basis of property, the many argue that decisions should be made on the basis of number. Taken to extremes, both definitions of justice promote inequality and injustice and incline regimes towards tyranny. In Aristotle's arrangement, the few and the many decide among themselves what is best before coming together to make a joint decision. As the many outnumber the few, decisions by the few would have to be supported by a large segment of the many in order to be implemented. And although the many outnumber the few, they often would be forced to build coalitions with the few in order to achieve their political goals. Aristotle admits that his idea is easier proposed than formalized because human nature tends to undermine even the most rational of plans.

VI. 4–5

If politics cannot operate smoothly along the lines of mathematical argument as proposed by Aristotle at the end of chapter 3, perhaps the wisest alternative is to manage the types of people who inhabit the city. Aristotle argues that the best sort of democracy is the one filled with a multitude whose main occupation is farming. Farmers have little property, little leisure and little desire to practice politics. Because they find farming more pleasant than politicking, they work their own land rather than work to dispossess others. And while there is always the chance that men living in democratic political societies might be corrupted by material pleasures, it is advantageous if citizens work rather than compare their stead to others. Aristotle posits that the few and the many might be satisfied if the multitude have a say politically yet leave governance of society to the wealthy or to the most capable.

The second best form of democracy is composed of herdsman. Like farmers, they are too busy trading to involve themselves in the trappings of politics. Moreover, the demands of the job put herdsman in an excellent position to defend the regime militarily.

The worst democracies are filled with men of limited means who, with a great amount of time on their hands, use their leisure to assemble and create dissension within the political community. Aristotle warns that if not tempered by more rural elements, urban democracies quickly fall apart.

The challenge for democratic political leaders is to guard against the wrong types of men becoming too prominent. For if the multitude far outnumbers the meritorious or the middling elements within a city, licentiousness eventually overruns a regime. Retaining more stringent citizenship requirements and remaining aggressively intolerant of the baser elements of society helps inoculate democracies against this malady.

Here once again Aristotle notes how difficult it is to recognize the dangers of allowing a regime to become overrun by baser elements within the city. In addition to remaining vigilant about the city's make-up, less stable democracies should encourage the creation of local associations, promote private and civic organizations, and in general, advocate (as the authors of the American Constitution would propose some two millennia later) political diversification to help prevent the majority from tyrannizing over society. In sum, Aristotle argues that democratic leaders cannot tolerate everything if by tolerating everything, immoderation is allowed to gain a foothold within the city.

In the spirit of recommendations he makes throughout Book V, Aristotle posits that the most important consideration for a democratic or an oligarchic regime is to engineer stability through moderation. As democracies become more democratic or oligarchies become more oligarchic, cities suffer, and sometimes fall apart.

One way that popular leaders of Aristotle's time destroyed their regimes is by confiscating property from the wealthy and redistributing it to the many. Another means they used to amass power was to pay out monies gained in foreign ventures to the people. Aristotle shows that when the multitude, even within a prosperous regime, becomes habituated to receiving, they always ask for more (hence Aristotle's description of this type of democratic arrangement as a 'punctured jar'). What should be done with the spoils of prosperity is to prop up the multitude so that it is not overly poor. Such an economic policy would include providing the poor with a means to work, granting the poor privileges to use public wealth commonly, and in the case of a democratic regime with large foreign holdings, by sending the poor out to subject cities where they would have greater opportunity to become wealthy. In essence, Aristotle advises that democratic rulers most benefit the regime not by giving in to the demands of the multitude but by enacting policies that aim to transform the multitude into men of the middling sort.

VI. 6–7

As democracy is best reformed by restraining elements within it that pervert freedom, oligarchies benefit when orderliness is put into the service of enfranchising as many in the city as possible.

What keeps oligarchies alive and well is their organizational skill. Here note that instead of distinguishing oligarchy from democracy based upon the standard of wealth, Aristotle highlights one of the more positive attributes of oligarchic rule. Unlike democracies that benefit (particularly regarding their defence) from their considerable populations, oligarchs, well outnumbered, tend to order their affairs well. Perhaps this explains why much of what Aristotle writes about oligarchy in this regard is explained within a military context.

Of the four elements of military power – the cavalry, the heavy-armed, the light-armed and the naval/seafaring, the strongest oligarchies are those whose country is suitable for horses. The precondition of an extensive countryside provides an explanation as to why men living within this regime would not only be able to become expert horsemen, but also as to why the multitude would have little opportunity over such a broad area to assemble and/or threaten the rule of the affluent.

Given that oligarchs will not always be so fortunately situated, Aristotle recommends that they work as much as possible to train heavy and light armed forces within their midst and to pay careful attention to the military education of their sons. In general, the more versatile the oligarchic regime, the greater the likelihood it will be able to secure itself.

On the political front, Aristotle advocates that oligarchs subsidize magnificent sacrifices for the city at large. In sum, the affluent should attempt to convince the many that they have their well-being in mind. What better way for oligarchs to establish their bona fides than to use their wealth? Aristotle notes that oligarchs in his time, however, have done nothing of the sort because they care more about gaining spoils for themselves than ruling in a dignified manner. To their political detriment, democratized oligarchs conceive of their worth solely in numerical (monetary) rather than aristocratic terms.

VI. 8

Aristotle discusses the offices that are necessary within the city in the last chapter of Book VI. In line with his recommendation that oligarchs secure their regime by arranging their affairs well, Aristotle posits that some offices help produce order within society. A rule to follow when considering offices is to consider the size of the city. Most cities need individuals overseeing markets, public works, natural resources, the treasury and records. The most difficult, yet necessary, office to fill is that office which oversees and executes justice. Aristotle notes that while the best men do not enjoy minding the judicial affairs of others, it is critical that the city prevent self-indulgent types from manning this office.

In line with what he writes about maintaining oligarchies, Aristotle comments that it is critical that competent types oversee military matters. Aristotle also advises cities to devote resources to religious officials, buildings and ceremonies. As regimes must be ordered well to survive, it follows naturally that regimes encourage public morality by tending to the city's gods. Aristotle's final remark on the subject of the arrangement of offices is that prosperous cities often take special care to institute managers of the affairs of women, children, gymnastics and Dionysiac contests. Aristotle merely observes that this is the custom among these types of cities, perhaps more cautious in the context of securing democracies and oligarchies of embarking upon a discussion that Socrates takes up controversially in the *Republic*.

CONCLUSION

Aristotle begins Book VI by attempting to arrive at the proper definition of freedom. Freedom rightly construed encourages both full participation of the deserving in the city's affairs and the opportunity to enjoy the fruits of political liberty. Aristotle ends Book VI by cautioning cities to arrange their offices aright. At the front and back end of Book VI, Aristotle teaches that the best democracies and oligarchies are guided by the understanding that the regime must balance the equally important political demands of freedom and order. The worst democracies and oligarchies tend in the direction of worst type of tyranny because they define freedom and orderliness in strictly numerical terms (i.e. 'Is my personhood or wealth valued regardless of what I merit?') to the detriment of freedom, order and thus the regime itself.

Aristotle's more encouraging rendering of democracy and oligarchy accounts for variants and mixtures of each and leaves open the possibility that democratic and oligarchic rulers might govern with an eye both to maintaining equilibrium between the demands of freedom and order and understanding the necessary place for each within political communities. If correct, Aristotle's account necessitates a further re-examination of Socrates' claim in the *Republic* that all things give way to the determining principle within both oligarchy and democracy to their ultimate corruption into the worst kind of tyranny. As most existing regimes fall somewhere in between the democratic and oligarchic spectrum, Aristotle's coverage suggests that moving forward, it is critical that statesmen learn how to balance the requirements of freedom and orderliness, rather than neglect one or the other out of hand ideologically.

STUDY QUESTIONS

1. What are the assumptions, beliefs and practices of democracy, as they are identified in Book VI, chapter 2? What are regarded as the defining principles of the regime?
2. What sort of justice 'is agreed to be democratic'?
3. According to Aristotle, what is the best sort of democracy? Why?
4. What happens to a regime if the multitude far outnumbers the notables and the middling elements? Why?
5. Do practices or policies that make democracies more democratic, and oligarchies more oligarchic, help preserve those respective types? Why or why not?
6. What does Aristotle say popular leaders of his time do to win the favour of the people?
   Cite two examples. Does he endorse what they do? Why or why not?
7. What provision in a democracy is like 'the [proverbial] punctured jar'? Can this practice be improved upon? If so, then

how so? If not, then why not? Can the notables play a role in such improvement, or is their existence at the root of the problem?

8. What kind of oligarchy is 'very close to so-called polity'? What other sort of regime is it related to? Why?

9. Why is a country suitable for horses apt for instituting a strong oligarchy?

10. What specifically should oligarchs do when they enter office? Why?

11. Do oligarchs of Aristotle's time do the above? Why or why not? Why are regimes led by such men like 'small democracies'?

12. Among the offices necessary to every city, which one is most necessary but also most difficult? Why is it difficult?

13. Which sort of offices are also necessary but require more experience and trust?

14. Should a city necessarily devote resources to religious officials, buildings and ceremonies?

15. What offices are peculiar to prosperous cities? Does Aristotle merely observe, or also recommend, them?

Politics VII

INTRODUCTION

Book VII is best divided into five parts. In chapters 1–3, Aristotle discusses the best way of life, arguing that individuals and cities must understand what is choice worthy in order to become happy. Aristotle's investigation into the merits of the 'active and political way of life' in the introductory section is pivotal to his overall consideration of the best regime as he continually revisits the pros and cons of political engagement, especially as it involves virtuous human beings, throughout Book VII.

Regimes need equipment, people, territory and suitable geography in order to be established. But Aristotle cautions his readers in chapter 4–7 that the best regime is not made happy simply by possessing advantages with regard to any of these provisions. Rather the happiness of the city is dependent upon the accompaniment of virtue, an ingredient provided by the excellence of its citizens. Aristotle proposes how cities might best be divided in terms of class, occupation and territory in chapters 8–12.

Of particular importance is his suggestion that the virtuous should enjoy the fruits of their goodness as their efforts most contribute to the city's happiness. Aristotle also introduces a power-sharing arrangement with the hope of preserving peaceful relations among prospective rulers. At the end of this section, however, Aristotle cautions that any attempt to ensure the city's happiness through the prudent administration of external goods is misdirected if one does not recognize the role that fortune plays in external matters.

In chapters 13–15, Aristotle describes how citizens might be educated towards virtue. Most importantly, legislators must organize their system of political education with insight as to the proper ordering of those things concerning the body, the appetite and the intellect. Aristotle discusses marital relations, offspring and early education in chapters 17–18.

VII. 1–3

Aristotle argues at the beginning of Book VII that comprehending the most choice-worthy way of life best enables students of politics to envision the ideal regime. Aristotle leaves the discussion of whether the most choice-worthy way of life is best for all in common or for individuals separately for later in his presentation.

Aristotle's starting point for establishing the most choice-worthy way of life is to separate the good things of this world into three groups – external goods, goods of the body and goods of the soul. He asserts that while there is little disagreement about what types of good things fall into these categories, people dispute which type of good is most desirable relative to the others. For Aristotle there is little doubt that the way of life accompanied by virtue is most choice worthy because men are able to 'acquire' and 'safeguard' external goods and bodily goods by virtuous living whereas neither external goods nor bodily goods procure the happiness associated with virtue. Using a formulation that Aristotle employs throughout Book VII, possession of a virtuous soul provides the best means to, and the best actualization of, human happiness whereas possession of external things and bodily goods cannot facilitate happiness and sometimes distract men from pursuing the best ends.

At best, external things are useful instruments. However most men incorrectly equate the accumulation of external things with happiness. This habit prevents them from choosing the best life as they instead attempt to acquire possessions instead of attaining virtue. Aristotle submits that like all instruments, external things have their limits, and produce trouble when possessed in excess. Whereas the soul can never become too virtuous, the possession of too many bodily and external goods can turn humans away from pursuing the best life. Furthermore, Aristotle implores his readers to judge the value of external things, bodily goods and virtue in relation to one another. Aristotle posits that in doing so, men recognize that it is not only better to be virtuous than to possess these other things but that the difference between the relative worth of each is astounding. Aristotle asserts that the clearest proof of this assertion comes from recognizing that the Gods are 'happy and blessed' without possessing any of these things.

The best way of life is the same for the city as it is for the man. Aristotle ironically uses the possession of wealth to make this point, arguing that those who use wealth as a measure judge it equally valuable to both the city and man. Yet his example simply proves that most men use the same standard when measuring the happiness of individuals and cities.

While it may be true that some assert that individuals and cities are happy on account of virtue, Aristotle's presentation in chapter 1 suggests that most judge happiness in terms of the possession of bodily or external things. Thus while it may very well be that virtuous cities are happy, political audiences in general need more convincing. For little in Aristotle's analysis up to this point assures the reader that most men are up to judging this matter rightly and to committing themselves and their cities to virtuous living.

This perhaps explains why Aristotle turns to a different investigation – namely, whether those who believe that the life accompanied by virtue is the most choice-worthy way of life agree as to whether that life is primarily political or philosophic. As those who are 'most ambitious with a view to virtue' both in his day and former times answer the question differently, Aristotle uses their competing arguments to redirect the discussion away from the opinions of those who misjudge what is choice worthy for the individual and the city. At the same time, showing how the virtuous consider the most choice-worthy way of life enables

Aristotle to critique the common argument that happiness results from satisfying one's bodily desires or by accumulating external things.

Central to the dispute between those who argue for and against the active life of virtue is the question of whether 'manly' engagement with the world interferes or complements one's employment of virtue. Proponents of manliness argue that by entering political life, men are given a greater stage on which they can celebrate virtue. They submit that if the virtuous life is the most choice-worthy life, why is it a bad thing to engage the greatest possible number of men politically to the advantage of both virtue and men themselves.

Critics of active political engagement counter that virtue politicized soon becomes a means to the end of mastering others. Here Aristotle references a variety of more militaristic regimes whose example points to the corruption of virtue in the name of the public good. Particularly interesting given his comments at the end of Book VII is Aristotle's critique of the Spartan regime for educating their citizens first and foremost towards a conception of virtue that is militaristic in nature.

The reader is left wondering from this debate whether or not political activity always develops into the art of mastering others. Most convincing is the notion that men conditioned to act in accordance with a political standard will soon seek out recognition for their effort. In other words, is one's acquisition of personal happiness enough for living the virtuous life? Or do most individuals show themselves outstanding relative to others? If victors gain the spoils of public recognition, are political communities left with the spoil of virtue redefined as conquest?

While Aristotle's presentation suggests that this criticism is somewhat compelling, he counters that political expertise is not the same as expertise in mastery. Voyagers and patients willingly employ both pilots and doctors respectively because they recognize that consenting to another's rule is to their advantage. And if political expertise is requisite for the city's happiness, would it not be required that men of virtue willingly take part in the political process? The challenge for cities should be to try to convince the virtuous with political ambitions that the most excellent celebration of virtue (and individual glory associated with its employment) comes from ruling over free men rather than dominating others. Displays of courage, strength and military skill have their place in the city. But rulers must understand that by making a city good, they make a city happy.

For Aristotle, war, if not the highest activity of all, is a necessary and noble activity. Given that the world is a place where men are often deceived, form factions, debate as to who should rule, and in general struggle with one another politically, it would be foolish to think that political rulers could ignore the always present prospect of war. Legislators best tend to the threat of domestic strife by building political partnerships within a city that encourage citizens to live well and to be happy. Furthermore, legislators, in recognizing that no city is an island, must prepare citizens for the prospect of conflict beyond the city's borders by specific sorts of military training.

This discussion invites remarks as to how legislators should lead with respect to neighbouring peoples. Aristotle frames his answer to the question in terms of his previous coverage of whether the virtuous should live active lives. Those who argue that the virtuous should not hold political offices suggest that it is better to be free from political responsibilities and claim that it is impossible for those who engage in politics to remain virtuous. Politics, as it distracts and corrupts, enslaves the virtuous by keeping men from virtuous activity. By comparing the city and the individual, as Aristotle does throughout Book VII, it is easy to understand how a city that became too active (perhaps defined in terms of trade, foreign expansion, etc.) could be distracted from its own wellbeing and corrupted by matters peripheral to its happiness.

Yet since happiness is a sort of action, Aristotle must examine whether all political activities corrupt. If political activity unequivocally corrupts the virtuous, the virtuous are incapable of remaining so unless they disengage from all activity involving other human beings. Instead Aristotle posits that just and moderate men can involve themselves in politics virtuously as long as they remain just and moderate. Nothing necessitates that the just and moderate become like those who they rule over. The virtuous may remain virtuous even if they acquire political power. The best example of this type of political activity is when equals rule one another and are ruled in return.

But just as the virtuous should be free to actively pursue virtuous living by engaging in political activity, they also should be free to keep to themselves, as the life accompanied by virtue is not predicated upon engaging others. Sometimes the virtuous life amounts to engaging in thought or in study. Human actions need not act externally to be virtuous or to produce happiness.

Applying the same rule to political communities, Aristotle suggests that unaffected cities are not inactive; rather they simply choose to engage one another in domestic partnerships. A city might tend towards a common philosophic way of life to the degree that its citizens were self-examining. But it is also important to note, as Aristotle's steady critique of Sparta makes clear, that foreign disentanglement could also breed a form of insularity that was antithetical to freedom and virtue.

VII. 4–7

What should one pray for in a best possible regime, concerning the quantity and quality of citizens, territory and geography? While most people answer that one should pray for everything in droves, as should be apparent by now, Aristotle is critical of judging a regime's worth in quantitative terms. It is better to judge citizens, territory and geography as choice worthy using the measure of capacity rather than number. Aristotle writes that one would never judge a doctor (e.g. Hippocrates) by his stature. Why then would one use size as a determinant to judge the best regime?

As Aristotle stresses throughout Books IV–VII, most people form an opinion on political matters by counting because they equate numbers with power. More refined political thinkers, instead of assuming that bigger is better or worse, consider how the quality of things enable them to perform their functions correctly. Aristotle does not insinuate that numbers do not matter. More precisely, he argues that the quality of things determine whether one should pray for their abundance. It is with this orientation that Aristotle takes up the question of how much population, territory and so on is a good thing.

Every city needs people. But if the city is to be governed finely, rulers must be as able to manage a city's population as citizens are able to abide by the laws and share in the political arrangement. Aristotle in effect reiterates his suggestion from Book VI that the best administered democracies and oligarchies incorporate the defining principles of freedom and orderliness into their administration. A city that is too small will not be self-sufficient in terms of its having the requisite population of free men to defend itself. A city that is too large will become unmanageable because its leaders will be unable to command and judge the citizenry. Aristotle extends his prescription regarding the demographic make-up of the citizenry to account for the ideal size and geographical setting for the city. The city should be large enough to live liberally in peace yet small enough so that it can be attended to. As for its placement, cities should be close enough to the sea to benefit from their interaction with their neighbours yet should guard against excessive influence of foreign elements.

As for the character of a citizenry, Aristotle proposes that it is important that citizens are filled with spiritedness and thought and art. Northern Europeans, filled with spiritedness are free yet disorderly. Asians, filled with thought and art, are orderly yet enslaved. The Greeks, although they too tend in sub-groupings to embody one characteristic at the expense of the other, are unique in that their possession of spiritedness, thought and art has enabled them to govern and to be governed well relative to others. Aristotle's words read somewhat prophetic when he submits that should all of the Greeks fall under one political heading, they would be capable of ruling all. Alexander of Macedon's later political accomplishments aside, Aristotle submits that all legislators should attempt to habituate their citizens with the mixing of these important elements in mind.

It is fitting that Aristotle references Socrates' education of the guardians in the *Republic* at this juncture. Aristotle agrees with Socrates' assertion that the spiritedness of a warrior class often creates affection for the regime yet Aristotle is more open to the idea that such men might be educated to be more discerning towards foreigners and each other. In essence, Aristotle holds out the prospect that the spirited that defend regimes also might be endowed with thought and art, thus mitigating perhaps the struggle between the greater and lesser cosmopolitan elements within a regime.

VII. 8–12

Aristotle reminds his audience that the discussion of population, territory and geography aside, the true mark of the best regime is the political orientation of its citizens towards virtue.

The city, like a house, is made well when all of its parts complement each another in the best possible way. Cities are more or
less well constructed on the basis of the number of those within
the regime who actualize virtue and the degree to which they are
able to do so.

Cities require material, instruments, arms, funds and religious
institutions. But the most necessary ingredient of a city's happiness is political judgement regarding what is just and advantageous in terms of relations between its citizens. Aristotle discusses
social class and function in chapters 8–12 with the aim of eluci-
dating the most virtuous composite of the city's parts given the
aforementioned requirements.

Aristotle begins with the admonishment that in the best
regime, citizens should not live a way of life that is antithetical to
virtue. Certain occupations such as farming, while providing for
a city's sustenance, should not be taken up by those whose main
concern is encouraging the city to be virtuous.

But as for the most important tasks, such as generalship and
political rule, Aristotle proposes an arrangement in which the
different people would perform these functions at the most
appropriate time of their lives. It is better to leave those matters
requiring force to the most virtuous among the young and to
give political power to those of the virtuous whose seasoning has
enabled them to become prudent. Here once again Aristotle
envisions an arrangement in which the requirements of spiritedness on the one hand and art and thought on the other are met
to the advantage of the political community.

Readers are left wondering, however, as to how this arrangement would work. What prevents the more spirited among the
virtuous from seeking dominion at home and abroad? What
ensures that the spirited will become less so as they advance in
age? Is it not imaginable that alliances might be formed between
young generals and elder rulers? Aristotle's proposal prompts
the reader to reconsider the merits of mixing virtue and political
activity.

This perhaps explains why much of Aristotle's discussion in
chapters 9–12 considers the distribution of possessions in connection with the holding of offices. Aristotle, unlike Socrates in
the *Republic*, authorizes the city to distribute possessions based
upon merit. Much as the vulgar should not be assigned offices

beyond their natural attributes, they should not share the rewards for performing the most important functions of the city. Given that Aristotle also addresses religious institutions in this segment of the text, perhaps the ultimate reward of old age is to be appointed to the priesthood. Worn out with the things of this world, priests enjoy peacefully contemplating heavenly things.

Thus central to the discussion of social functions in the best regime is the question of who gets what in the city. As to the division of the city's territory, Aristotle posits that the city be partitioned into four parts: territory held in common for public service to the Gods, territory held in common that is utilized for the common messes, territory held by private parties within the city proper and territory held by private parties at the city's frontier. One overarching consideration and two more specific concerns guide Aristotle's suggested partition of the city. In general, all division of property should be made with the character of the citizenry in mind. As to common lands, Aristotle suggests that it is important that citizens are attached to the Gods and one another. Of more concern related to the division of private property is that citizens be assigned property both within the city and at the frontier. Aristotle's hope is that by giving private parties a stake in geographically diverse sections of the city, faction might be warded off.

Aristotle makes other provisions concerning the physical configuration of the city. Cities should be positioned well relative to natural elements such as the sun, wind and water supply. Furthermore, it is not an unmanly thing if cities use artificial fortifications to secure themselves against foreign enemies. Better to use art to complement virtue than to think that safeguards weaken a city's standing with prospective invaders.

As for developing associations among citizens, Aristotle posits that it is essential that rulers divide the public square into a 'free' market kept clear of trade, vulgar people and farmers and a common or necessary market that is suitable and convenient for exchange between producers and consumers. The purpose of the free market is to have a place in the city that engenders respect and fear within the citizenry. Important office holders, priests and military types would use this arena to strengthen ties between men of diverse, yet highly regarded occupations. The common market would serve as a place where all other necessary associations within the city could be performed. Aristotle adds that the division between free and common markets should be duplicated in the country, thereby suggesting once again that it is vital that the city's physical arrangements be uniform so as to encourage broad devotion to the city.

VII. 13–15

Aristotle's detailed plan for organizing a city's territorial, market and sociological infrastructure might persuade the casual reader that he thinks that a city can be made happy through intelligent policy. Yet Aristotle reminds his audience that it is foolish to believe that the best laid plans of political thinkers are realizable simply by writing them down on paper. Instead, setting out such an arrangement is as much a work of prayer as it is of invention and the actualization of such a city is more a matter of chance than design.

Yet all is not lost for political communities if leaders turn their attention back to the regime. For by ordering regimes rightly, political rulers can increase the likelihood that their cities will be happy. The work of ordering a regime rightly is not a matter of prayer or of chance but of intentional and correct choice concerning the city's primary end of happiness and the best means of accomplishing this objective. While Aristotle notes that leaders often get it wrong on both of these fronts, he leaves open the possibility that practitioners of the science of politics can develop an understanding of politics that improves the well-being of cities. In order to be successful, leaders must bear in mind that the practice of virtue is essential to attaining happiness. Regardless of rewards or hardships that are associated with all human activity, virtuous living always produces happiness.

As Aristotle noted at the beginning of Book VII, most men consider happiness to be a matter of acquiring external things. And legislators rightly pray for the materialization and augmentation of external things. Yet the city's excellence cannot be a matter of fortune if its excellence is measured by the virtue of its citizenry. In other words, as is it possible for legislators to induce citizens to be excellent, a city's happiness depends upon their efforts to educate men towards excellence.

What makes a city excellent is its citizens being excellent. Simple enough. But according to Aristotle, how do citizens become excellent? Aristotle answers that it is best for citizens to be excellent individually. Aristotle hedges on the likelihood of all to becoming excellent as a grouping yet delves into how individual men can become excellent through nature, habit and reason. Aristotle submits that by nature, men develop as individual human beings. As men grow, their habits influence their nature for better or for worse. What makes human life unique is that human beings may be taught to employ their reason through persuasion. Thus given that human beings are capable of reasoning, it is not futile to attempt to educate them politically.

Aristotle's handling of the subject of political education is made complicated by the fact that political communities consist of both rulers and ruled. As political education requires leadership, Aristotle first considers the questions of who should rule and for how long. Given that men do not differ from one another to the same extent as they differ from Gods and heroes, the general rule is that men who are similar to one another should rule and be ruled in turn.

Fortunately for the legislator, the customary respect for one's elders and the realization that each will have the opportunity to rule later in life makes possible a system in which older men rule over younger men. As was the case earlier when Aristotle assigned different roles to the virtuous, the natural differentiation among human beings based upon their biological age comes to the rescue of the regime attempting to be virtuous. Aristotle's attempt at political education thus rests upon the presupposition that men can acquire the best life if they are willing to pursue their political ambitions within an arrangement in which they first must be ruled.

As the city is divided between old and young, the human soul is also divided into two parts, reason and that part able to follow the rule of reason. Aristotle's political education regarding the constitution of the individual and 'life as a whole' boils down to the simple premise that 'the worse is always for the sake of the better'. If men can be convinced that the most choice-worthy elements within their soul and within society should rule, men have the opportunity to become happy.

The problem, as has been highlighted by Aristotle throughout his commentary on politics, is that men in general, even when they are willing to consider the question of good government, usually accept the argument that the most choice-worthy life is the life of aggrandizement, domination and conquest. Oddly enough, as is shown best in the case of the Spartans, men seek mastery over others thinking that dominance will make them happy. Yet to argue as Aristotle does – namely, that the worse is always for the sake of the better, is not to endorse the enslavement of the worse but to promote an understanding of the right ordering of things both to individuals and to political communities.

In Aristotle's day, the Spartans, keen on educating their young, are mistakenly praised as models of good legislators because they sought to prepare their citizens to dominate those around them. Aristotle's alternative model is of a form of political education that does not teach men to master others more than it instructs them to rule over free men as they would wish to be ruled themselves. The Spartan model proves effective in war but much less effective in peace. If war itself is a means to the enjoyment of the peace, the Spartan example shows how people can be reduced to unhappiness by focusing their efforts on military success rather political happiness.

Here it is helpful to reference the preamble to the United States Constitution of 1787. Americans form a new union not to dominate others but to 'insure domestic tranquility' and 'provide for the common defense' so as to best 'secure the Blessings of Liberty'. The United States of America in part represents the actualization of Aristotle's idea of a regime oriented towards the enjoyment of peace through the establishment of a reasonable political arrangement that encourages both freedom and order.

Aristotle recognizes that men can orient their laws, priorities, education and economy so as to best acquire happiness yet still undergo political adversity. For as no political community and no citizen is an island, both the city and man must contend with the realization that dangers might arrive at any moment. Possessing the virtues of moderation, courage and endurance on the one hand, and philosophy and justice on the other enable the best city and the best man to achieve happiness regardless of good or bad fortune. Moderation, courage and endurance supply cities and men with the necessary defence against cowardice during times of war. And philosophy and justice enable men to enjoy their happiness during times of peace.

Aristotle notes that the Spartan regime properly conditioned its citizens to be courageous, moderate and resilient during times of war but did not teach its citizens how to enjoy their leisure virtuously. Without a political education complemented by philosophy, the Spartans failed to make good use of the excellent things of life while at peace. As has been Aristotle's mantra throughout Book VII, the Spartan regime that lived by the sword died by the sword because it is unable to distinguish the worse from the better. Rather the Spartans prepare for war while at peace, limit their leisure to tend to their military pursuits, and practice altruism for the solitary sake of political survival.

Importantly, Aristotle does not suggest that Spartan discipline in and of itself is a bad thing. But returning to a distinction he makes earlier in Book VII, it becomes clear that the Spartans misconstrue what is best for their city. Namely, they fail to take up properly the question of what order the body, the appetite and the intellect should be superintended or educated so as to further the city's happiness. Aristotle submits that as men develop from birth to adulthood, their bodies should be superintended before their souls, and their appetites should be superintended before their intellects. But as 'the worse is always for the sake of the better' and reason, not material survival, is the highest end of our nature, a city's system of political education must be structured for the sake of the employment of virtue. Therefore while all things must be done with the betterment of the bodily development of the individual and the city in mind, it is philosophic orientation that in the end will determine the degree to which it is truly a blessed place.

VII. 17–18

Aristotle's discussion in Book VII closes with his investigation into how the bodies of citizens might be habituated to their ideal state. He first proposes that procreation be organized around human life expectancy. In terms of safe delivery, the quality of human stock and safeguarding public mores, men in their mid-thirties ideally would mate with women 18 and older for 15–20 years. Aristotle also proposes exposing deformed children, allowing abortion in some instances, and regulating the diet, activities and care of children with a watchful eye up until the age when their education might 'supply that element that is lacking in nature'.

STUDY QUESTIONS

1. What is the most choice-worthy way of life?
2. Is the most choice-worthy way of life the same for a man as it is for a city?
3. What question do men who agree upon the most choice-worthy way of life nonetheless answer differently? Why?
4. Why does it make 'no small difference on which side the truth lies' with respect to the above question?
5. What way of life is believed by some to be the only one for a real man?
6. What is the only way to be politically active according to most men? How do their regimes relate to neighbouring regimes? What is the goal or orientation of their laws?
7. What specific response does Aristotle give to the above view?
8. What is the responsibility of the legislator with respect to neighbouring peoples? In connection with what other responsibility or task?
9. How does Aristotle answer the question referred to in #3 above? What points does he make to support his answer?
10. Does his answer pertain to both individuals and cities? Explain.
11. Based on what Aristotle says in chapters 4–6 and 11, what might he say about the geographical expanse of, for example, the United States, its number of citizens and immigration?
12. What are the positive and negative aspects of 'spiritedness' on the one hand, and of 'endowment with thought' on the other? Why should citizens possess both?
13. What is 'the cause of there being several kinds and varieties of city and several sorts of regime'?
14. What are the necessary components of a city? What is 'the most necessary thing of all'?
15. In the best regime, what ways of life should citizens avoid? Why?
16. In the best regime, should the same men defend and govern the city? Explain.
17. In the best regime, how should territory be divided? Why?
18. Is a city's happiness or excellence dependent on chance?

19. What makes a city excellent?
20. On account of what three things do men become good and excellent?
21. How should men who are equal or similar in virtue rule themselves? Why?
22. What natural distinction facilitates that manner of rule? Explain.
23. Explain Aristotle's statement that 'the worse is always for the sake of the better' in regard to the constitution of the individual and 'life as a whole'. Is the explanation politically relevant?
24. What virtues should be present in a city?
25. In what order should the body, the appetite and the intellect be superintended or educated?

Politics VIII

INTRODUCTION

Book VIII, the last and shortest book of the *Politics*, concerns not, or rather not primarily, the education of adult citizens, as do many prior parts of the *Politics*, but the education of the young. That should be the foremost concern of the legislator, Aristotle says. Hence the end of the *Politics* establishes the focal point of politics; and its brevity, perhaps, its non-negotiability.

The book moves from the general question of the nature of excellence to that of the means to attain it, the subject of most of the book. Excellence entails leisure, by which Aristotle means not merely free time or recreation, but mindful engagement, akin perhaps to the liberal arts; for such reflective engagement cultivates judgement, essential to a life lived well, as well as to political virtue or ruling. Hence the education of children should approximate and thus prepare them for a lifetime of reflection, a thoughtful life. That approximation and preparation chiefly involves music. Because not all kinds of music cultivate a disposition for reflection, however, crafting a programme of early education requires knowledge of the various kinds of music and of their respective effects on the soul – in other words, requires both musical expertise and philosophy. By inference, then, if the foremost concern of a regime should be the souls of its children, then its legislators and rulers should have musical and philosophic souls.

VIII. 1–4

Although Aristotle begins by noting that education should cultivate the character peculiar to a given regime so as to secure it, as if to say that the culture of a regime should harmonize with its political structure – a democratic culture or character with a democracy, for example, he notes that there are better and worse characters, as if to say that harmony or political excellence should not forsake excellence as such.

If, then, excellence is an end for the city as a whole, education should be common not private, that is, 'one and the same for all'.

What sort of public education is best? Chapter 2 raises the question whether education should be practical, moral or intellectual. In other words, should education cultivate good citizens or extraordinary human beings? Book VII's debate over the superiority of the philosophic and political ways of life appeared to settle the question in favour of philosophy, at least for adults. Focusing now on children, Aristotle says that they should learn useful and necessary tasks and arts, but only those that are 'free' not those that are 'unfree' or slavish and will make them vulgar, that is, unable to engage in virtuous habits and actions. Vulgar activities resemble work for wages, inasmuch as they weaken the mind, making it unsuitable for study – or leisure properly understood, which children should also engage in, up to a point, so as not to harm their health. Study simply for the sake of proficiency rather than for enjoyment or virtue paradoxically has the effect of vulgar activities, weakening or injuring the body.

More specifically, chapter 3 informs us, children should learn how to write and draw as well as engage in gymnastics; the latter not only maintains health and vigour but develops courage. Early education should also incorporate music not, as might be assumed, merely for recreation or rest, but to cultivate a disposition to study or use leisure well.

A discussion of leisure ensues, one which suggests that the matter concerns not only education for children but activities suitable for free persons. Leisure (the Greek word for which '*schole*' is the root of 'scholarship') involves 'pleasure, happiness, and living blessedly'. Unlike occupation, which is undertaken for an end, leisure is an end in itself. To put the point in contemporary idiom, leisure constitutes an alternative to a life of work punctuated by vacations. And if Homer's Odysseus counts as authoritative, then music – specifically listening to a singer – is the best sort of leisure.

Aristotle closes chapter 3 by declaring obvious that education of the body must precede education of the mind, and education in habits must precede education through reason, thereby introducing the topic of chapter 4, physical education.

Addressing the topic of the extent and purpose of physical education, chapter 4 recalls the earlier discussion in chapter 2 of Book VII that distinguishes the political way of life from mastery, domination and tyranny. Gymnastic, sports and other sorts of physical training can be both overdone and underdone. Too much emphasis on them impedes growth, causes injuries and cultivates tendencies towards aggression and conflict, whereas too little makes children timid. The aim of exercise should rather be courage and nobility; not a disposition to pick fights but a willingness to fight for honourable reasons. The disposition of a lion, not of a wolf. Thus although Aristotle mentions that misguided physical training may harm young bodies, he maintains focus on its effects on the souls or characters of children.

VIII. 5–7

Chapter 5 examines music in earnest: What is its power? For the sake of what – play, rest or virtue? If virtue, then does music affect disposition as does gymnastic the body? (Yet chapter 4 indicated that gymnastic affects disposition too.) Or does music even affect the mind?

Another question is should boys play, or only listen to, music? If they devote themselves to playing, then the music will be better than if they do not take it seriously. But if that argument holds, Aristotle says, then they should also devote themselves to cooking – a strange conclusion! In other words, the issue isn't how to make *music* best, but how to make *boys* best, involving the same issue as whether music affects character or mind. To suggest that Zeus play and sing the lyre for the sake of the poets would be vulgar.

It would appear, in answer to the question, that music has the power to entertain as well as to improve the mind and character. As entertainment, it is restful and thus pleasant; improving the mind involves the also pleasurable element of nobility, which music has. Accordingly we all claim that music belongs to the category of the most pleasant things and expect it at social gatherings. While the pleasure music yields seems to justify its inclusion in the education of children simply because it adds pleasure to learning, a better justification for its inclusion would be its power to relieve the pain and exertions of learning, for then it would be more nearly a necessary accompaniment. Whether as added pleasure or relief, however, music masks the end of education and induces some persons to mistake pleasure for that end and even for the end of life.

Moreover, it's evident from the inspirational effect of music that it does not merely complement but instead constitutes education, for inspiration is a passion connected with character. By affecting our character or soul, music has the power to influence judgement; rhythms and tunes evoke emotions or states of mind such as anger, calm, courage and moderation, which either prevent or foster our recognition and enjoyment of respectable characters and noble actions. Such recognition and enjoyment virtually makes us respectable and noble.

The extent of music's power over our soul becomes even more evident when contrasted with other perceptible things – what can be touched, tasted or seen, for example. Among those things, only visible things – shapes and colours – can indicate character or disposition. Here, in the middle of chapter 5, Aristotle distinguishes but leaves fused two points. One concerns the capacity of those things that affect our senses to depict character or disposition: while the soft fur of a rabbit and the sour taste of a lemon do not indicate qualities or traits of character, a sketch, painting or sculpture can indicate bravery, compassion, fury, dignity or deceit, for example. Yet even depictions of brave, compassionate, furious or wicked men do not inspire bravery, induce compassion, incite anger or entice evil – that is, alter our very disposition. At least, Aristotle adds, not to the degree music can. The second point thereby emerges: (visible) images in comparison to (audible) sounds illustrate that the capacity to depict qualities or traits of character is not unrelated to their capacity to move us. We apprehend, recognize or 'get' such qualities or traits the more we feel them, and we feel them more through sounds than through sights. (Hence to enhance the experience of listening to music, listeners sometimes close their eyes.) Because paintings and sculptures may affect children somewhat, the images they are exposed to should depict good or noble actions and qualities of character. Nonetheless, most attention should be paid to what moves them more, namely the kind of music they hear.

At the end of chapter 5, Aristotle thus analyses a number of ancient musical modes or styles: in particular Mixed Lydian, Dorian and Phrygian. The first makes listeners sad or anguished, the second calm and collected, and the third inspired and passionate. The capacity of music to move the soul, which in itself gives pleasure, makes it a fitting component of a child's education, for children do not tolerate what does not please them.

Addressing the question of whether children should play and sing or just listen to music, chapter 6 begins with two arguments in favour of the former: active participation makes them better judges of music and also keeps them occupied, answering to their need to be occupied. Aristotle regards the arguments as conclusive, prompting only the question of the age at which children should play instruments and sing. Since the aim is culti-vation of judgement, playing and singing should be undertaken at a young age. Once judgement is cultivated – the capacity to distinguish noble from frenzied tunes, for example, having laid the foundation for political virtue – youth can stop their music education. An extended education in music, or maintaining pro-ficiency, does risk one's capacity to engage in other activities, including military and political endeavours, which require strength and stamina. Hence the musical education of children should not aim for professional results; they should neither enter competitions nor even attempt the extravagant feats of execu-tion promoted by them. At the same time, as has been estab-lished, children should not merely enjoy music. They should learn to recognize and appreciate good music without becoming entertainers.

The goal of music appreciation requires exclusion from a child's education of instruments that do not cultivate good musical taste, in particular the flute and stringed instruments. Music from the flute tends to be frenzied and thus appropriate only for dramatic performances seeking a cathartic rather than educational effect. The flute also prevents singing. Enthusiasm for the flute dates to the proliferation of leisure in Greece characterized by pursuit of all the arts and sciences without discrimination, an enthusiasm abandoned after experience proved the inappropriateness of the flute for the cultivation of virtue. Stringed instruments had a similar history. Legend says that Athena threw away the flute she invented because it distorted her face; more likely she did so, Aristotle says, because flute playing does not engage the mind. Apparently the demands of playing the flute and stringed instruments, the technical skill and physical dexterity, impede appreciation of the music itself.

The last chapter of the book, taking up the question of which kinds of harmonies and rhythms are suitable to education, refers those who want a detailed answer to experts in music and in philosophy, and claims only to identify distinctions recognized in practice and to venture a general discussion.

In practice, the division of tunes into three categories by philosophers guides the use of music. According to that division, tunes relate to character, to action or to inspiration, and each kind conduces to one of three ends, namely, education, catharsis and relaxation. Music for the young, focused on their education, should employ tunes that best express character; by contrast choruses in dramatic performances for adult citizens, focused on their catharsis or emotional release, should employ tunes evoking action and inspiration. By inducing, for example, pity and fear, choruses calm an audience by purging them of passions. Such release harmlessly delights. Music intended simply to delight, entertain or relax should be directed only towards uneducated audiences comprised of labourers, mechanics and the like, and consist of colourful, strained harmonies – deviations like the souls of the spectators.

Socrates of *The Republic* should not therefore have recommended chromatic Phrygian tunes, along with Dorian, for education. Frenzied and passionate, Phrygian tunes excite listeners as much as the flute. By contrast, grave Dorian tunes inspire fortitude. Hence tributes to the God Dionysus, as were ancient dithyrambs, cannot employ Dorian modes, as Philoxenus's failed

composition of *The Mysians* illustrated. Relative to other harmonies, then, Dorian ones fall in the middle between extremes
and are thus the most suited to schooling children.

STUDY QUESTIONS

1. What are the components of a good education for children?
   Why?
2. What is 'leisure'?
3. How does the discussion of physical education in chapter 4
   complement the discussion of the political way of life in
   chapter 2 of Book VII?
4. Should education involve 'music'? What sort of music?
   Why?
5. Should students play music, listen to it or both? Why?

CHAPTER 4

RECEPTION AND INFLUENCE

INTRODUCTION

How did Aristotle's contemporaries react to the political commentary of the *Politics,* and how did his successors react to it in the centuries after its appearance? This chapter takes up those questions.

Three aspects in particular of Aristotle's political views challenged the prevailing views of his culture: (1) his claim that cities are natural and changeable by men to fulfil their purposes challenged the view that cities are gifts from the Gods and their fates thus subject to the Gods; (2) Aristotle's claim that the function of cities is to promote virtue challenged the democratic Athenian view that their function is to maximize freedom and (3) his view that cities should go to war only for the sake of peace (a condition of the pursuit of virtue) challenged the ancient view that cities should go to war for the sake of victory and conquest (in other words, Aristotle reconceived the traditional view of manliness). Those of his contemporaries who opposed the constant warfare of Greek cities and who constituted an emerging 'Quietist' movement accordingly welcomed his views, whereas others were vexed by them.[1]

I MARCUS TULLIUS CICERO (106–43 BC)

Between the death of Aristotle in 384 BC and the appearance of the works of Cicero in the middle of the first century BC, the evolution of political philosophy stalled or, at any rate, survives only in fragments. That fallow period makes Cicero's contribution all the more valuable inasmuch as it may accumulate, refine or extend speculative moves made during that time – the three centuries before the Christian era known as the Hellenistic age and constituting a transition from the ideas of Greece to those of Rome.[2] The importance of Cicero lies also in the considerable part he played in the revival of Aristotle's works.[3] Indeed, at the start of his treatise *On Obligations*, Cicero admits the philosopher's great influence on him: worried about his son Marcus's progress under the tutelage of a teacher in Athens, Cicero recommends to Marcus his father's works and says, they 'do not differ markedly from those of the Peripatetics, for both they and I aspire to be followers of Socrates and Plato – you must exercise your own judgement on the content without pressure from me'.[4]

While Cicero compliments Aristotle's 'marvelous breadth of knowledge',[5] he credits him most for his views on oratory and cites several times, in his own treatise *Orator*, Aristotle's *Rhetoric* and *Topics*.[6] Cicero nonetheless criticizes philosophy as a whole when he notes the stark distinction between it and the art of public speaking:

> [Philosophers] converse with scholars, whose minds they prefer to soothe rather than arouse; they converse in this way about unexciting and non-controversial subjects, for the purpose of instructing rather than captivating . . . gentle and academic . . . their style lacks the vigour and sting necessary for oratorical efforts in public life . . . it has no equipment of words or phrases that catch the popular fancy; it is not arranged in rhythmical periods, but is loose in structure; there is no anger in it, no hatred, no ferocity, no pathos, no shrewdness; it might be called a chaste, pure and modest virgin.[7]

Not surprisingly, then, unlike Aristotle Cicero does not rank philosophical virtue supreme but instead, consistent with his esteem for oratorical skill, the political art.[8] The statesman applies the highest virtue within the best form of government, a composite of monarchy, aristocracy and democracy. Cicero's theory of the state and statesmanship, presented in the form of two dialogues entitled *On the Commonwealth* and *Laws*, may in particular reflect those speculative moves of the Hellenistic age alluded to above that alter the course of political philosophy, for the perfect statesman or king patterns his conduct upon that of God and embodies law and 'true law – namely, right reason . . . is in accordance with nature, applies to all men, and is unchangeable and eternal'.[9]

If rulers rule impartially according to right reason, not giving priority to utilitarian or other considerations, then the state would embody a universal principle of justice common to all humanity: 'It will not lay down one rule at Rome and another at Athens, nor will it be one rule today and another tomorrow. But there will be one law, eternal and unchangeable, binding at all times upon all peoples'.[10] In this respect, Cicero's conception of the state prefigures the idea of a universal society founded on moral conceptions intrinsic to political liberalism.[11]

Statesmen up to the challenge of god-like universalistic rule do not however need to believe in God as such – they can be sceptics like Cicero[12] – but they do need belief in honour and duty to country. Indeed, in *On Obligations* Cicero concludes that honour is either the only or the highest good, invokes Aristotle for support, and connects honour to the useful:

> If we are born to embrace the honourable, and this must either be our sole pursuit (as Zeno thought) or at any rate must be accounted to have immeasurably greater weight than all else (as Aristotle argues), then the necessary conclusion is that the honourable is either the sole or the highest good. Now what is good is certainly useful, and so whatever is honourable is useful.[13]

Moreover, like Aristotle, Cicero believed that human law should encourage not only honour among citizens but also their pursuit of happiness.[14] Hence Cicero retains some Aristotelian values while moving political philosophy towards later developments, such as natural law and divine right.

II SAINT AUGUSTINE (354–430)

The first notable Christian political thinker, St Augustine of Hippo, dismissed Aristotle in favour of Plato. In his voluminous – over one-thousand page work – *The City of God*, he devotes only a single paragraph to Aristotle, and only to give double-edged praise:

> The reason for my choice of the Platonists, in preference to all others, is that the reputation and prestige they enjoy above the rest is in proportion to the superiority of their concept of one God, the creator of heaven and earth. The judgement of posterity has rated them far above other philosophers; how

far is shown by the sequel. Aristotle (a disciple of Plato and a man of commanding genius, no match for Plato in literary style, but still far above the general run), founded a school called the 'Peripatetics' (the name being derived from his habit of walking about while discussing) and, thanks to his brilliant reputation, attracted to his sect a large number of disciples, even in the lifetime of his teacher. After Plato's death, his nephew Speusippus and his favourite disciple Xenocrates succeeded him in his school, which was called the Academy, and they and their successors were hence called the 'Academics.' In spite of this, the most notable philosophers of recent times have rejected the title of 'Peripatetics' or 'Academics,' and have elected to be called 'Platonists'.[15]

So much for Aristotle!

III ALFARABI (870–950), AVERROES (1126–1198) AND MAIMONIDES (1135–1204)

Like St Augustine, Muslim and Jewish medieval political philosophers also confronted the problem posed by the appearance of Greek philosophy within their religious communities: namely, at least apparent conflict between the demands of divinely revealed law and faith, on the one hand, and those of reason and philosophical inquiry, on the other. Not all of them however resolved the conflict as St Augustine did, by making philosophy the handmaiden of theology, the means by which to articulate and explain, to the extent possible given the weak power of reason, an omnipotent monotheistic God, His ways, and the way to Him through faith in Jesus Christ. While some non-Western thinkers indeed saw the conflict as significant and the only solution the dominance of one over the other, others saw it as marginal and their incorporation possible. Accordingly, they estimated differently the practical difficulties of a simultaneous commitment to a particular religion and to the human mind, and likewise to divine authority and to conventional authority.

Non-Western philosophers who contributed to this debate contributed also, in the process, to a reinvigoration of Aristotle's philosophy. For the most part, however, they did not write systematic treatises on the usual topics of political philosophy – such as law, justice and government – and they did not focus as much on Aristotle's *Politics* as on his works on logic, metaphysics and ethics.

Likewise the founder of Islamic political philosophy, Alfarabi, who wrote *Aphorisms of the Statesman*, *The Philosophy of Plato* and *The Virtuous City*. Known as 'the second teacher' – the second most important philosophical source after Aristotle – Alfarabi, who taught in Baghdad when it was the cultural centre of Islam, helped integrate Western philosophy into the Islamic world by addressing the new problem it revealed, namely, how should political life accommodate revealed religion? Drawing on both Plato and Aristotle, Alfarabi said political order should bring about happiness, the health of the soul, through statesmanship; hence the statesman needs knowledge of both the soul and politics. Knowledge of the soul reveals its most venerable part, the intellect, which knows divine matters, 'becomes cognizant of the Creator', and thereby magnifies His majesty.[16] Embodied within a sensible soul, the intellect thus connects man to God and to nature:

> [the soul] is like an intermediary between the intellect and nature, for it possesses natural senses. Thus it is as though it were united at one end with the intellect, which is united with the Creator according to the approach we have mentioned, and at the other end with nature, which follows it in density but not in location.[17]

Able to know a changeless God, the soul is immortal. Hence Plato's and Aristotle's cognitive theory, according to Alfarabi, was right: learning is recollection. Alfarabi thus simultaneously (1) subordinates the intellect, and its powers of reason and philosophy, to the divine, (2) validates reason and philosophy, (3) indicates Aristotle's likeness to Plato and (4) reaffirms the accepted divine aspect of Platonism.[18]

Indeed, Alfarabi tries not only to show the compatibility or unity of the claims of reason and those of revelation, but also in so doing to harmonize Plato and Aristotle. He regarded their differences as superficial and believed their views on logic, generation and ethics to be virtually identical. They agree, for example, that God made the world and patterned what he made on (divine) forms; otherwise everything brought into existence would have been brought into existence haphazardly. And they both believed in 'recompense for good and evil actions'.[19]

In brief, by arguing Aristotle's harmony with Plato, and Plato's with Islam, Alfarabi sought to prove a necessary connection between Western philosophy and Islamic religion.

A few centuries after Alfarabi, however, Aristotle, at least in the eyes of another Islamic philosopher by the name of Averroes, trumped Plato. For although in addition to his numerous commentaries on Aristotle Averroes wrote one on Plato's *Republic*, he said Aristotle possessed 'the ultimate human mind'. Latin scholars in turn respected the mind of Averroes: during the thirteenth to the mid-seventeenth centuries they routinely read Aristotle along with his commentaries.

Responding to the challenge to Islamic beliefs posed by Greek philosophy, Averroes wrote a treatise arguing that the Koran mandates philosophy by way of its injunction to reflect on God's design. Averroes' own reflection on that design led him to conclude, against the claims of Islamic philosopher Avicenna (980–1037), that divine causal necessity not random contingency created the world. That is, God ordered eternal matter: 'it is God, Blessed and Exalted, who is the Maker, Giver of being, and Sustainer of the universe; may He be praised and His Power exalted!'[20]

The eternal world, made by a pre-eternal being and thus not preceded by time, indicates the coincidence of worldly matter with time, but thereby raises the question, Are past and future time finite or infinite? Dialectical theologians such as Plato and his followers, according to Averroes, hold that, while future time and future being are infinite, past time and past being are not; by contrast, Aristotle and his school hold that both past and future time and being are infinite. Averroes points out that infinite time-and-being 'bears a resemblance . . . to the pre-eternal Being'. At the same time, he acknowledges that it is not the same, since eternal matter is caused and perishable, while the pre-eternal Being is neither. Apparently, both Platonic and Aristotelian views bear truth. 'Thus', Averroes concludes, 'the doctrines about the world are not so very far apart from each other that some of them should be judged as constituting unbelief and others not'.[21]

Against Alfarabi's and Averroes' eternalism, the Jewish philosopher Maimonides argued that Aristotle's arguments for eternity were not demonstrative but rather metaphysical projections of potentiality. Nonetheless, although assertion of the world's eternity in fact denies God, Maimonides maintains its rhetorical or exoteric value inasmuch as 'eternal' means changeless, everlasting and incorporeal – all attributes of God. In his masterpiece *Guide of the Perplexed*, he first points out the problem with eternalism and then explains why it is a 'true opinion . . . of immense importance': 'if the world were created in time, there would be a deity; and if it were eternal, there would be no deity'. However, Maimonides says, the former cannot be demonstrated, only claimed, whereas the latter indicates a deity:

> If . . . the world is eternal, it follows necessarily . . . that there is some being other than all the bodies to be found in the world; a being who is not a body and not a power in a body and who is one, permanent, and everlasting; who has no cause and who cannot change: this, then, is the deity. . . . For this reason you will always find me . . . establishing [the existence of the deity] by arguments that tend toward the eternity of the world, not because I believe in the eternity of the world, but because I wish to establish in our belief the existence of God, the Exalted, through a demonstrative method as to which there is no dispute in any respect.[22]

Indeed, according to Maimonides, physically healthy human beings are naturally constituted to seek knowledge of God:

> that individual obtains knowledge and wisdom until he passes from potentiality to actuality and acquires a perfect and complete human intellect and pure and well-tempered human moral habits. All his desires are directed to acquiring the science of the secrets of this existence and knowledge of its causes, and his thought always goes toward noble matters, and he is interested only in the knowledge of the deity and in reflection on His works and on what ought to be believed with regard to that. His thought is detached from, and his desire abolished for, bestial things. (I mean the preference for the pleasures of eating, drinking, copulation, and, in general, of the sense of touch, which Aristotle explained in the *Ethics*,

saying that this sense is a disgrace for us. How fine is what he said, and how true it is that it is a disgrace! For we have it only in so far as we are animals like the other beasts, and nothing that belongs to the notion of humanity pertains to it . . .).[23]

A well-governed city, according to Maimonides, will impart this model of human living to its citizens, steering them towards happiness and away from misery 'by training their moral habits to abandon what are only presumed to be happiness so that they not take pleasure in them and doggedly pursue them'. In addition, rules of justice – nomoi – should order their associations. Hence Maimonides recommends to his contemporaries works of ancient philosophy to correct deficiencies in the manner in which rulers rule: 'On all these things, the philosophers have many books that have been translated into Arabic, and the ones that have not been translated are perhaps even more numerous. In these times, all this – I mean the regimes and the nomoi – has been dispensed with, and men are being governed by divine commands'.[24]

IV SAINT THOMAS AQUINAS (1225–1274)

St Thomas Aquinas was as generous with his attention to and praise of Aristotle as the earlier Christian, St Augustine, was stingy. When Aristotle's works were rediscovered in the thirteenth century and translated into Latin (first by William of Moerbeke), after having been lost or unread in the Western world, the Dominican friar Thomas devoted his life to them, rigorously arguing their compatibility with Christianity. By contrast, Thomas's peers, a Catholic community of scholars, denounced Aristotle's treatises as the works of a 'pagan' – a man who lived centuries before the birth of Jesus, provoking a reaction similar to that provoked by Darwin's *Origin of the Species* in the nineteenth century. Challenging their denunciation, Thomas set out to prove that Aristotle's arguments are compatible with Roman Catholic beliefs, which yielded his voluminous and unfinished *Summary of Theology*.

While much of that work repeats Aristotle's arguments in the *Politics* to show their logical superiority to arguments of earlier philosophers and theologians, its integration of religious and theological tenets expose the challenge of St Thomas's project of reconciliation. In particular, his conception of natural law, constitutive of strict moral prohibitions immune from circumstances, appears at odds with Aristotle's conception of natural right, constitutive of moral considerations attentive to circumstances. In addition, St Thomas's allowance of capital punishment of recalcitrant heretics, gives more civic influence to priestly judgement than Aristotle recommends.[25] Hence scholars debate whether or not St Thomas's effort convincingly demonstrates the compatibility of faith, or revelation, and reason, or succeeds only to reveal a tension between a life guided by one and a life guided by the other. In any case, St Thomas reintroduced Aristotle into Western thought and made sure that his arguments could not be easily dismissed by Christianity.

V DANTE ALIGHIERI (1265–1321) AND MARSILIUS OF PADUA (1275–1342)

Although not known for his politically relevant work, Dante Alighieri, author of the *Divine Comedy*, deserves brief mention here for his lesser read *De Monarchia* (ca. 1312). Like St Thomas, Dante drew extensively from Aristotle while fashioning a Christian interpretation of political life. Unlike St Thomas, however, Dante maintains the need for a world government more authoritative than the Pope: specifically, a monarchical empire, justified by the monarch's direct receipt of authority from God.[26]

Also like St Thomas Aquinas, Marsilius of Padua presents himself as a follower of Aristotle, whom he calls 'the divine philosopher' or 'the pagan sage'. Indeed, his work *The Defender of Peace* (1324) reads like a medieval appendix to the *Politics*. He explicitly agrees with Aristotle that the purpose of the commonwealth is to secure the good life, which life is characterized by the engagement of the practical and speculative virtues. And he agrees that metaphysical speculation is superior to political activity.[27]

But Marsilius's central concern was the political rule of priests or papal power. He is both critical of and excuses Aristotle for not addressing the gravest disease of civil society, the assumption of political authority by the clergy. Of course Aristotle could not have witnessed this disease, for it was the consequence, albeit accidental, of the miracle of Christian revelation. Marsilius says that he will deal with this and only this disease because Aristotle has already analysed other serious political diseases.

Marsilius did not support the Church being the ultimate political authority and universal theological-political rule by the papacy. He denies that any religious authority – priest, bishop pope – has by divine right the power to command or coerce and to determine in a legally binding way what is orthodox and what heretical. Limiting the powers of the Church, he advocates increased secular political authority.

In conjunction with his political secularism, Marsilius distinguishes between political theology and political philosophy. In other words, he notes throughout his work the political teaching which is demonstrable from that which is not, inasmuch as it is revealed only by God. In the past, the answer to the question of political order has been given from the perspective of faith, not reason.

While Marsilius denounces the dogmatism of much medieval political thought, he does not denounce Christianity as such. He reserved his scepticism rather for those men who claim to be most knowledgeable about it. The people, not priests, should rule, and then only those citizens who are truly faithful – the original meaning of the church. To promote faith, divine laws should be promulgated. That promulgation is the proper function of priests. Moreover, according to Marsilius – disagreeing with Aristotle – that function surpasses in importance the activity of ruling. In this respect, Marsilius appears to be, like St Thomas Aquinas, a Christian Aristotelian.

VI MARTIN LUTHER (1483–1546) AND JOHN CALVIN (1509–1564)

Martin Luther, German monk, professor of philosophy at the University of Wittenberg, and leader of the Protestant Reformation, published in 1520 an address to the Christian nobility of the German nation alleging abuse of authority by the papacy. Included in his roster of complaints, criticism of university education and its teaching of the 'blind heathen' Aristotle, who misleads Christians on the subjects of nature, the soul and the virtues – subjects implicated in the *Politics* as much as in the works Luther names:

> Now, my advice would be that the books of Aristotle, the *Physics*, the *Metaphysics*, *Of the Soul*, *Ethics*, which have hitherto been considered the best, be altogether abolished, with all others that profess to treat of nature, though nothing can be learned from them, either of natural or of spiritual things. Besides, no one has been able to understand his meaning, and much time has been wasted and many noble souls vexed with much useless labour, study, and expense. I venture to say that any potter has more knowledge of natural things than is to be found in these books. My heart is grieved to see how many of the best Christians this accursed, proud, knavish heathen has fooled and led astray with his false words. God sent him as a plague for our sins.

Luther goes on to say that Aristotle erroneously teaches that the soul dies with the body and promotes virtues directly contrary to Christian ones ('Oh that such books could be kept out of the reach of all Christians!' he exclaims.)[28] Luther nonetheless approves inclusion in the university curriculum of Aristotle's *Logic*, *Rhetoric* and *Poetry*, to educate students in speaking and preaching.

The French theologian and religious reformer John Calvin held a view of Aristotle nearly opposite to that of Luther. While he venerated the liberal arts and in particular Greek and Roman oratory and philosophy, he moreover commended, in Plato, Aristotle and Cicero, whom he occasionally cited, 'the voice of reason'[29]:

> When God . . . wishes us to contemplate his works here before approaching him and participating in his image as we are intended to: if we profane all that and wish to know nothing, is it not manifestly to battle against our God to renounce the good that he wished to do us, yes, that which is the chief one and that most to be esteemed? . . . God has not put men in this world to deny them any intelligence, for he does not wish them to be like asses or horses, he has endowed them with reason and has wished them to understand.[30]

Calvin also endorsed Aristotle's idea of natural subordination and hierarchy:

> Those who cannot submit themselves to the magistrates, who rebel against their fathers and mothers, who cannot bear the yoke of masters or mistresses, sufficiently show that they cannot join with anyone who does not reverse the whole order of nature and jumble heaven and earth, as people say. [Furthermore,] anyone who has been established above others ought diligently to aim at improving them.[31]

Despite his commendation of reason and natural order, Calvin's expressed admiration for the classics exuded enthusiasm rather than sobriety:

> Read Demosthenes or Cicero, read Plato, Aristotle, or others of that crew: they will, I admit, allure you, delight you, move you, enrapture you in wonderful measure. Then betake yourself to that sacred reading.[32]

In his last years, Calvin put his enthusiasm for classical humanism into practice by establishing, as did Aristotle, an academy for future political leaders, albeit for clerics as well. Still, Calvin's commitment to the classics never superseded that to his faith and he criticized Aristotle in particular for crediting the order of nature and natural endowments rather than God's providence with actualities and potentialities; according to Calvin, the former are instruments of God and not his only ones. While Aristotle 'excelled in genius and learning' then, he professed according to Calvin 'many erroneous speculations'.[33]

VII FRANCIS BACON (1561–1626) AND THOMAS HOBBES (1588–1679)

Along with Machiavelli and Descartes, Francis Bacon and Thomas Hobbes founded modern thought by modelling the science of man – his epistemology and politics – on the new science of nature. Thanks largely to St Thomas Aquinas who rehabilitated Aristotle in the West in the thirteenth century, such later political philosophers, who sought to introduce novel ideas, had to dispute not only the political claims of Christianity (chiefly, the divine right of kings) but also those of Aristotle.

Bacon wanted to accomplish man's dominion over nature and complained that Aristotle merely trafficked in words – perfecting syllogisms, creating categories and criticizing theories. Aristotle thereby undermines physical evidence and practical arts by supplanting 'the voice of nature' with 'the voice of dialectics'. In short, he 'corrupted the philosophy of nature' by divorcing it from things and deserting experience.[34]

Furthermore, Bacon thinks that his contemporaries are 'far ahead' of Aristotle 'in precedents, in experience', and 'in the lessons of time' – with respect not only to natural philosophy but also to military and political science.[35]

Bacon does not however confine his criticism to points of doctrine. His polemical essay, 'The Refutation of Philosophies', claims Aristotle 'was of an impatient and intolerant cast of mind . . . perpetually concerned to contradict, hostile and contemptuous of the past, and purposely obscure. Many other qualities also he had which smack of the school-master, not of the researcher into truth'.[36]

The mid-seventeenth century Englishman Thomas Hobbes, although he does not write a scathing review of Aristotle's character, also like Bacon harshly criticizes Aristotle's metaphysical reading of nature and its political implications. According to Hobbes's masterwork, *Leviathan,* the only directive or purpose that nature gives human beings is the fear of violent, unexpected death, which he thinks each individual spontaneously translates via reason into the imperative: do what you must to preserve your own life. Given that fundamental self-interestedness of each man, a collective agreement among a community of men to establish an authority in exchange for security is the most rational course of action for them to take. Individual self-preservation thus motivates the creation of a social contract, and reveals itself to be the end – and not as Aristotle thinks simply the beginning or condition – of collective life.

VIII JEAN-JACQUES ROUSSEAU (1712–1778) AND ADAM SMITH (1723–1790)

Jean-Jacques Rousseau concurs with Hobbes that natural man has an instinct for self-preservation, again a belief not in itself at odds with Aristotle. But Rousseau, also like Hobbes but unlike Aristotle, believes that man is naturally solitary. Accordingly, neither speech nor a sense of justice develops in natural man. Hence in order for man to live in society, he must change. Society, or a polity, does not result from man's natural propensities and attributes as Aristotle says, but rather from a series of accidents that bring men together and change their very natures in the course of doing so. That changed nature can then deliberately create a society that enables him to preserve his individual will, if not recapture his original freedom, albeit via a collective, general will.

A general will depends on frequent assembly and equal recognition of citizens; inequalities cannot be the basis of institutions and rights. Indeed, Rousseau accuses Aristotle of elitism, though inaccurately inasmuch as he ignores Aristotle's distinction between oligarchy and aristocracy and thereby fosters a class analysis of Aristotle's political views still seen today. Rousseau nonetheless acknowledges Aristotle for distinguishing public from private economy and like him maintains that societies should be small and have proportional features.[37]

In comparison to his contemporary Rousseau, Adam Smith shares more views with Aristotle, albeit in reference more to Aristotle's ethics than to his politics. In *The Theory of Moral Sentiments*, in which Smith describes ethical conduct as conduct monitored by an 'impartial spectator' – an internal point of view that regards the self and others objectively in the context of circumstances – he acknowledges Aristotle's contribution in *The Nicomachean Ethics* to the relevant concepts of propriety and moderation. Similarly, he cites approvingly Aristotle's *Poetics* on the appropriateness of certain measures of verse to expression of certain sentiments and passions. By contrast, Smith disapproves of Aristotle's justification in the *Politics* of abortion in cases of deformities and in circumstances of overpopulation, both considerations of public utility.[38]

IX EARLY AMERICAN STATESMEN (1783–1790)

Even the Founding Fathers of the American political system consulted Aristotle. In 1783, prior to the writing of the US Constitution in 1787–1788, James Madison included Aristotle's *Politics* among a list of books he recommended for congressional use.[39] Although scholars debate the extent of early American statesmen's knowledge of and reliance on classical sources, several conclude that the republican theory of government they devised reflects ancient political insights and constitutional principles. The best evidence of Aristotle's direct influence on the newly proposed form of government appears in the writings of John Adams, whose *A Defence of the Constitutions of Government of the United States of America*, published in 1787, not only deems a republic a better model of government than a democracy, but quotes Aristotle's *Politics*, establishing that Adams read it 'carefully and critically'.[40]

While critical of Aristotle's ideal regime, Adams derives from Aristotle's concept of polity or the best regime for most circumstances, three conditions of liberty: the rule of law, a politically enfranchized middle class, and mixture of aristocratic, oligarchic and democratic elements. All three ward off unchecked political influence and domination by any one person or group. At the same time, he regarded rule by an unvirtuous mob a threat to liberty.[41]

Likewise, *The Federalist Papers*, by Alexander Hamilton, James Madison and John Jay, recommend the republican form to help cure the diseases to which small democracies, such as those of ancient Greece and Italy, are prone.[42] In a republic, Madison writes in Federalist #10:

> [representatives] refine and enlarge the public views by passing them through the medium of a chosen body of citizens, whose wisdom may best discern the true interest of their country and whose patriotism and love of justice will be least likely to sacrifice it to temporary or partial considerations. Under such a regulation it may well happen that the public voice, pronounced by the representatives of the people, will be more consonant to the public good than if pronounced by the people themselves, convened for the purpose.

To ward off the possibility that representatives may betray the people, an enlarged sphere as opposed to a small one furnishes more individuals of better character from which to elect representatives: 'if the proportion of fit characters be not less in the large than in the small republic, the former will present a greater option, and consequently a greater probability of a fit choice'.[43]

Thus, like Aristotle's mixed regime, albeit without explicit credit to him, the Founders' republican design encourages virtuous leadership in the context of political liberty.

In 1790, Federalist James Wilson chose to quote Grotius about Aristotle:

> Among philosophers, Aristotle deservedly holds the chief place, whether you consider his method of treating subjects, or the acuteness of his distinctions, or the weight of his reasons. I could only wish that the authority of this great man had not, for some ages past, degenerated into tyranny, so that truth, for the discovery of which Aristotle took so great pains, is now oppressed by nothing more than by the very name of Aristotle.[44]

Other Founders however, such as Thomas Jefferson, express more ambivalence about Aristotle.[45] Moreover, their use of Aristotle and other classical thinkers never replaces their own independence of thought.[46] Their voluminous writings and expansive debates answer the question Federalist #1 raises: societies of men *are* really capable 'of establishing good government from reflection and choice'.

X ALEXIS DE TOCQUEVILLE (1805–1859) AND JOHN STUART MILL (1806–1873)

In the year 1831, Alexis de Tocqueville, a descendant of French aristocracy and member of the court of Versailles, set off to America with a friend to study America's prison system and, impressed by the country's flourishing democracy, simultaneously began research for his voluminous tome, *Democracy in America*. Unlike Aristotle, who maintains that the character of a regime or government – whether democratic or otherwise – determines the way of life of citizens, Tocqueville concluded the reverse: a country's way of life, political culture or *moeurs*, determines the character of a regime – a view that also challenged Tocqueville's contemporaries, French intellectuals who thought ideology key to a successful regime. Cultivation of certain *moeurs* or mental habits in a citizenry preserves democracy; without them citizens become vulnerable to despotic tendencies of governments and ideologies.

Tocqueville also thought that, because the ancient democracies of Greece and Rome depended on inequalities of privilege and condition, those of superior rank within them did not believe and could not even imagine that all human beings are alike and equal. He may well have been critical of Aristotle in this respect:

> All the great writers of antiquity were a part of the aristocracy of masters, or at least they saw that aristocracy established without dispute before their eyes; their minds, after expanding in several directions, were therefore found limited in that one.[47]

Yet many observations – too numerous to include all here – throughout the paradoxical *Democracy in America*, endorse aristocratic values by way of endorsing freedom as a counter to too much equality; where freedom reigns, distinctions among persons will necessarily result. Such distinctions can also in turn promote freedom, as in the case of lawyers, whom Tocqueville says form a distinctive class among the educated because of the knowledge they acquire, and serve the people by protecting, and instructing the people about, their individual rights:

> Men who have made the laws their special study have drawn from their work the habits of order, a certain taste for forms, a sort of instinctive love for the regular sequence of ideas, which naturally render them strongly opposed to the revolutionary spirit and unreflective passions of democracy. . . . The body of lawyers forms the sole aristocratic element that can be mixed without effort into the natural elements of democracy and be combined in a happy and lasting manner with them . . . without this mixture of the spirit of the lawyer with the democratic spirit . . . I doubt that democracy could long govern society, and I cannot believe that in our day a republic could hope to preserve its existence if the influence of lawyers in its affairs did not grow in proportion with the power of the people.

By serving on juries the people, Tocqueville explains, learn judicial language, the laws and their rights – which protect individual liberties from incursions by the spirit of the multitude or will of the majority.[48] Indeed, although Tocqueville does not cite Aristotle, he too points out throughout *Democracy in America* the despotic tendency of the opinion of the many over the opinion of the few.

Tocqueville also reveals his aristocratic side when he praises classical education despite his belief that 'scientific, commercial, and industrial' education better serves the social and political needs of democracies:

> There is no literature that puts the qualities naturally lacking in the writers of democracies more in relief than that of the ancients. Thus there exists no literature better suited for study in democratic centuries. That study is the most fitting of all to combat the literary defects inherent in these centuries . . . Greek and Latin ought not to be taught in all schools; but it is important that those whose nature or whose fortune destines them to cultivate letters or predisposes them to that taste find schools in which one can be made a perfect master of ancient literature and wholly steeped in its spirit. To attain this result, a few excellent universities would be worth more than a multitude of bad colleges where superfluous studies that are done badly prevent necessary studies from being done well.
>
> All those who have the ambition to excel in letters in democratic nations ought to be nourished often from the works of antiquity. It is a salutary diet.[49]

In sum, while Tocqueville admired modern democracy in America, he believed that certain aristocratic values and features would strengthen it by enabling freedom and excellence to check oppressive equality and mediocrity.

Like Tocqueville, John Stuart Mill thinks that democratic republics are vulnerable to the tyranny of the majority, in particular 'social tyranny . . . the tyranny of the prevailing opinion and feeling'.[50] Their vulnerability derives from their fierce adherence to the principle of equality, which breeds pressure to think and act like others. The pressure to conform results in turn in collective mediocrity. Thus, like Aristotle, Mill thinks that democracy undermines excellence. In *On Liberty*, Mill tries to foster excellence by emancipating the individual from societal pressures to conform, with 'one very simple principle': no one, whether individually or collectively, may interfere with the liberty of action of anyone else except for self-protection. That principle of liberty extends, Mill argues, to thought and speech. The maximization of freedom guarantees that individuality will flourish and better ideas and conduct will emerge.[51] In *On Utilitarianism*, Mill also wants to promote 'the greatest good for the greatest number'. While human beings weigh 'good' in terms of their pleasure or happiness, they differentiate higher from lower pleasures and prefer the former. Thus Mill adopts Aristotle's science of character, which argues that happiness depends on self-control of impulses and activities that challenge our minds. Unlike Aristotle, however, Mill does not admit that such happiness or greatest good may not be shareable by the greatest number, or that the prevalence of individuality does not assure the prevalence of excellence.

XI KARL MARX (1818–1883)

No question, Karl Marx admired Aristotle: 'the greatest thinker of antiquity', 'the most encyclopaedic intellect of them', he said. Nonetheless, he discards as well as incorporates Aristotelian claims. For example, Marx's novel historical conception of nature as process – the coming-to-be of nature and man through human labour – rejects all non-historical conceptions as abstractions, and even though it retains a teleology, it is an historical dialectic like Hegel's, not an individualistic metaphysics like Aristotle's. According to Marx, systems of labour or production, or in other words various sorts of economies, purge their material contradictions over time through revolutionary conflicts, until human labour becomes entirely free – spontaneous and un-coerced. The resulting community of workers works for the pleasure of working, not out of necessity or with the aim of stockpiling goods. Hence Marx's critique of capitalism also gives credit to Aristotle in two respects. First, to his distinction between 'oeconomic' and 'chrematistic': acquisition of useful goods or money for exchange versus acquisition of superfluous goods and accumulation of money beyond its use as a medium of exchange – the first being thus limited and the other, unlimited. Second, in order to explain the paradox of exploitation under capitalism, credit to Aristotle's observation that even time-and-labour saving tools, like shuttles that weave cloth, need operators: the more efficient machinery is, the greater the incentive to maximize productivity by lengthening the working day. In sum, while Marx and Aristotle disagree about the nature of the world and of human beings, they agree that productivity for the sake of accumulation alienates rather than fulfils man.[52]

After Marx, there emerged more mixed and complicated twentieth-century responses to Aristotle. Some of these adapt Aristotle's thought to contemporary agendas, deliberately omitting or replacing some of his arguments.

XII LEO STRAUSS (1899–1973), HANNAH ARENDT (1906–1975), MICHAEL OAKESHOTT (1902–1990) AND JOHN RAWLS (1921–2002)

Four twentieth-century political philosophers helped to generate renewed interest in Aristotle in the 1970s by appropriating his ideas in various ways: which one represents him best? Leo Strauss captures the paradoxes of Aristotle's thought – its foreign and familiar, commonsensical and philosophical, and ancient and modern, aspects and incorporates into his own thought in particular the idea of 'natural right' traceable to both Plato and Aristotle. Hannah Arendt champions Aristotle for identifying public life as key to human flourishing. Michael Oakeshott employs Aristotle – along with Hobbes and Hegel – to articulate his concept of 'civil association', an ideal condition undistracted by historic ambiguities. And John Rawls invokes 'the Aristotelian Principle' to account for 'primary goods': because human beings prefer challenging activities equal to their capacities, rather than easier ones, they deserve the conditions requisite to engaging in them – namely, rights and liberties, opportunities and powers, and income and wealth. A just society, then, secures those conditions of human flourishing.[53]

Modifying Rawls to address resulting disparities of development among persons, Martha C. Nussbaum (1947–) along with economist Amartya Sen, propose policies designed in particular to empower women in poor non-Western countries. In contrast to that policy-oriented employment of Aristotle, Alasdair MacIntyre (1929–) thinks that Aristotle's political ideals are inaccessible to the modern world because they are contextually dependent on a particular constellation of community.[54] These examples give merely a sample of the myriad ways Aristotle has been interpreted and, as all provocative secondary literature does, compels the reader to return to the *Politics* itself, to verify or refute proposed interpretations.

CHAPTER 5

GUIDE TO FURTHER READING

I RECOMMENDED EDITIONS AND TRANSLATIONS OF THE *POLITICS*

Politics. Trans. Ernest Barker. Oxford: Clarendon, 1968.
—. Ed. Alois Dreizehnter. Studia et Testmonia Antiqua VII. Munich: Wilhelm Fink Verlag, 1970.
—. Trans. Carnes Lord. Chicago: University of Chicago Press, 1984.
—. 4 vols. Ed. W. L. Newman. Oxford: Clarendon, 1887–1902. Rpt. Arno Press, 1973.
—. Trans. H. Rackham. Loeb Classical Library, 1944.

II GENERAL COMMENTARIES ON THE *POLITICS*

Barker, E. *The Political Thought of Plato and Aristotle*. New York: Dover, 1959.
Barnes, Jonathan. *Aristotle*. New York: Oxford University Press, 1982.
Bien, Günter. *Die Grundlegung der politischen Philosophie bei Aristoteles*. Frieburg/Munich: Verlag Karl Alber, 1973.
Coby, Patrick. 'Aristotle's Four Conceptions of Politics'. *Western Political Quarterly* 39, no. 3 (1986): 480–503.
Cooper, John M. *Reason and Human Good in Aristotle*. Indianapolis: Hackett, 1986.
Davis, Michael. *The Politics of Philosophy: A Commentary on Aristotle's Politics*. Lanham, MD: Rowman & Littlefield, 1996.
Frank, Jill. *A Democracy of Distinction: Aristotle and the Work of Politics*. Chicago: University of Chicago Press, 2005.
Gadamer, Hans-Georg. *The Idea of the Good in Platonic-Aristotelian Philosophy*. Trans. P. Christopher Smith. New Haven: Yale University Press, 1986.
Grene, Marjorie. *A Portrait of Aristotle*. Chicago: University of Chicago Press, 1963.
Jaffa, Harry V. 'Aristotle'. In *History of Political Philosophy*. 2nd edn. Ed. Leo Strauss and Joseph Cropsey. Chicago: University of Chicago Press, 1972. pp. 64–129.
Keyt, David. 'Three Fundamental Theorems in Aristotle's Politics'. *Phronesis* 32, no. 1 (1987): 54–79.
Kraut, Richard. *Aristotle: Political Philosophy*. Oxford: Oxford University Press, 2002.

Lord, Carnes. 'Aristotle'. In *History of Political Philosophy*. 3rd edn. Ed. Leo Strauss and Joseph Cropsey. Chicago: University of Chicago Press, 1987. pp. 118–54.

—. 'The Character and Composition of Aristotle's *Politics*'. *Political Theory* 9, no. 4 (1981): 459–78.

Morall, John B. *Aristotle*. London: George Allen & Unwin, 1977.

Mulgan, Richard. *Aristotle's Political Theory: An Introduction for Students of Political Theory*. Oxford: Clarendon, 1977.

Pellegrin, Pierre. 'La "Politique" d'Aristote: Unité et fractures éloge de la lecture sommaire'. *Revue Philosophique de la France et de L'étranger* 177, no. 2 (1987): 129–59.

Randall, John Herman, Jr. *Aristotle*. New York: Columbia University Press, 1960.

Riedel, Manfred. *Metaphysik und Metapolitik: Studien zu Aristoteles und zur politischen Sprache der neuzeitlichen Philosophie*. Frankfurt am Main: Suhrkamp Verlag, 1975.

Ritter, Joachim. *Metaphysik und Politik: Studien zu Aristoteles und Hegel*. Frankfurt am Main: Suhrkamp Verlag, 1969.

Romilly, Jacqueline de. *La loi dans la pensée grecque: Des origines à Aristote*. Paris: Société d'Édition 'Les Belles Lettres', 1971.

Ross, W. D. *Aristotle: A Complete Exposition of His Works and Thought*. New York: Meridian, 1959.

Salkever, Stephen G. *Finding the Mean: Theory and Practice in Aristotelian Political Philosophy*. Princeton: Princeton University Press, 1990.

Schmidt, James. 'A Raven with a Halo: The Translation of Aristotle's *Politics*'. *History of Political Thought* 7, no. 2 (1986): 295–319.

Simpson, Peter L. Phillips. *A Philosophical Commentary on the 'Politics' of Aristotle*. Chapel Hill, N.C.: University of North Carolina Press, 1998.

Smith, Steven B. 'Goodness, Nobility, and Virtue in Aristotle's Political Science'. *Polity* 19, no. 1 (1986): 5–26.

Strauss, Leo. 'On Aristotle's Politics'. Chapter 1 in *The City and Man*. Chicago: University of Chicago Press, 1964.

Swanson, Judith A. *The Public and the Private in Aristotle's Political Philosophy*. Ithaca: Cornell University Press, 1992.

Voegelin, Eric. *Plato and Aristotle*, vol. 3 of *Order and History*. Baton Rouge: Louisiana State University Press, 1957.

III THE RELATION BETWEEN ETHICS AND POLITICS

Adkins, A. W. H. 'The Connection between Aristotle's *Ethics* and *Politics*'. *Political Theory* 12, no. 1 (1984): 29–49.

Aristotle. *The Nicomachean Ethics*. Trans. David Ross. Rev. ed. Oxford: Oxford University Press, 1980.

Bodéus, Richard. *Le philosophe et la cité: Recherches sur les rapports entre morale et politique dans la pensée d'Aristote*. Paris: Société d'Edition 'Les Belles Lettres', 1982.

Irwin, T. H. 'Moral Science and Political Theory in Aristotle'. *History of Political Thought* 6, no. 1/2 (1985): 150–68.
Vander Waerdt, P. A. 'The Political Intention of Aristotle's Moral Philosophy'. *Ancient Philosophy* 5, no. 1 (1985): 77–89.

IV THE THEME OF NATURE

Ambler, Wayne H. 'Aristotle's Understanding of the Naturalness of the City'. *The Review of Politics* 47, no. 2 (1985): 163–85.
Aristotle. *Metaphysics.* Trans. Hugh Tredennick. Cambridge: Harvard University Press, 1933, 1935.
Voegelin, Eric. 'What is Right by Nature?' In *Anamnesis.* Trans. and ed. Gerhart Niemeyer. Notre Dame: University of Notre Dame Press, 1978. pp. 55–70.

V THE HOUSEHOLD AND WOMEN

Booth, William James. 'The New Household Economy'. *American Political Science Review* 85, no. 1 (1991): 59–75.
—. 'Politics and the Household: A Commentary on Aristotle's *Politics* Book One'. *History of Political Thought* 2, no. 2 (1981): 203–26.
Clark, Stephen R. L. *Aristotle's Man: Speculations upon Aristotelian Anthropology.* Oxford: Clarendon, 1975.
—. 'Aristotle's Woman'. *History of Political Thought* 3, no. 2 (1982): 177–91.
Elshtain, Jean Bethke. 'Aristotle, the Public–Private Split, and the Case of the Suffragists'. In *The Family in Political Thought.* Ed. Jean Bethke Elshtain. Amherst: University of Massachusetts Press, 1982. pp. 51–65.
Fortenbaugh, W. W. 'Aristotle on Slaves and Women'. In *Ethics and Politics*, vol. 2 of *Articles on Aristotle.* Ed. Jonathan Barnes, Malcolm Schofield, and Richard Sorabji. London: Gerald Duckworth, 1977. Pp. 135–9.
Horowitz, Maryanne Cline. 'Aristotle and Woman'. *Journal of the History of Biology* 9, no. 12 (1976): 183–213.
Keuls, Eva C. *The Reign of the Phallus: Sexual Politics in Ancient Athens.* New York: Harper & Row, 1985.
Lacey, W. K. *The Family in Classical Greece.* Ithaca: Cornell University Press, 1968.
Loraux, Nicole. *Les enfants d'Athena: Idées athéniennes sur la citoyenneté et la division des sexes.* Paris: Francois Maspero, 1981.
Morsink, Johannes. 'Was Aristotle's Biology Sexist?' *Journal of the History of Biology* 12, no. 1 (1979): 83–112.
Saxonhouse, Arlene W. 'Family, Polity, and Unity: Aristotle on Socrates' Community of Wives'. *Polity* 15, no. 2 (1982): 202–19.
Swanson, Judith A. 'Aristotle on Nature, Human Nature, and Justice: A Consideration of the Natural Functions of Men and Women in the City'. In *Action and Contemplation: Studies in the Moral and Political*

Thought of Aristotle, ed. Robert C. Bartlett and Susan D. Collins.
Albany, NY: State University of New York Press, 1999. pp. 225–47.
—. Review Essay of *Feminist Interpretations of Aristotle*, ed. Cynthia
A. Freeland.*Ancient Philosophy* 20 (2000): 501–13.

VI SLAVERY, ACQUISITION AND PUBLIC ECONOMY

Ambler, Wayne H. 'Aristotle on Acquisition'. *Canadian Journal of
Political Science* 27, no. 3 (1984): 486–502.
—. 'Aristotle on Nature and Politics: The Case of Slavery'. *Political
Theory* 15, no. 3 (1987): 390–410.
Castoriadis, Cornelius. 'From Marx to Aristotle, from Aristotle to Us'.
Social Research 45, no. 4 (1978): 667–738.
Dobbs, Darrell. 'Aristotle's Anticommunism'. *American Journal of
Political Science* 29, no. 1 (1985): 29–46.
—. 'Natural Right and the Problem of Aristotle's Defense of Slavery'.
The Journal of Politics 56, no. 1 (1994): 69–94.
Finley, M. I. *The Ancient Economy*. 2nd edn. Berkeley: University of
California Press, 1985.
—. 'Aristotle and Economic Analysis'. In *Ethics and Politics*, vol. 2 of
Articles on Aristotle. Ed. Jonathan Barnes, Malcolm Schofield, and
Richard Sorabji. London: Gerald Duckworth, 1977. pp. 140–58.
Mansfield, Harvey C., Jr. 'Marx on Aristotle: Freedom, Money, and
Politics'. *Review of Metaphysics* 34, no. 2 (1980): 351–67.
Meikle, Scott. 'Aristotle and the Political Economy of the Polis'.
Journal of the Hellenic Studies 99 (1979): 57–73.
Nichols, Mary P. 'The Good Life, Slavery, and Acquisition: Aristotle's
Introduction to Politics'. *Interpretation: A Journal of Political Philos-
ophy* 2, no. 2 (1983): 171–83.
Polanyi, Karl. 'Aristotle Discovers the Economy'. In *Primitive, Archaic,
and Modern Economies: Essays of Karl Polanyi*. Ed. George Dalton.
Boston: Beacon, 1968. pp. 78–115.

VII CITIZENSHIP AND POLITICAL RULE

Collins, Susan D. *Aristotle and the Rediscovery of Citizenship*.
Cambridge: Cambridge University Press, 2006.
Develin, Robert. 'The Good Man and the Good Citizen'. *Phronesis* 18,
no. 1 (1973): 71–9.
Faulkner, Robert. 'The Gentleman-Statesman: Aristotle's (Compli-
cated) Great-Souled Man'. Chapter 2 in his *The Case for Greatness:
Honorable Ambition and Its Critics*. New Haven: Yale University
Press, 2007.
Frede, Dorothea. 'Citizenship in Aristotle's *Politics*'. In *Aristotle's
Politics: Critical Essays*. Ed. Richard Kraut and Steven Skultety.
Lanham, MD: Rowman & Littlefield, 2005. pp. 167–84.
Mansfield, Harvey C., Jr. 'Aristotle: The Executive as Kingship'.
Chapter 2 in his *Taming the Prince: The Ambivalence of Modern
Executive Power*. New York: The Free Press, 1989.

Mulgan, Richard. 'Aristotle and the Value of Political Participation'. *Political Theory* 18, no. 2 (1990): 195–215.

Schofield, Malcolm. 'Sharing in the Constitution'. *Review of Metaphysics* 49 (1995–1996): 831–58.

Swanson, Judith A. 'Prudence and Human Conduct: A Comparison of Aristotle and Oakeshott'. In *Vernunft und Ethik im politischen Denken Michael Oakeshotts.* Ed. Michael Henkel/Oliver Lembcke. Darmstadt: Wissenschaftliche Buchgesellschaft, 2009.

Zuckert, Catherine H. 'Aristotle on the Limits and Satisfactions of Political Life'. *Interpretation: A Journal of Political Philosophy* 2, no. 2 (1983): 185–206.

VIII JUSTICE, LAW, TYPES OF REGIME AND REGIME CHANGE

Brunschwig, Jacques. 'Du mouvement et de l'immobilite de la loi'. *Revue Internationale de Philosophie* 34, no. 133–34 (1980): 512–40.

Gagarin, Michael. *Early Greek Law.* Berkeley: University of California Press, 1986.

Kalimtzis, Kostas. *Aristotle on Political Enmity and Disease: An Inquiry Into Stasis.* Albany, NY: State University of New York, 2000.

Lindsay, Thomas. 'Aristotle's Qualified Defense of Democracy through "Political Mixing."' *The Journal of Politics* 54 (1992): 101–19.

MacDowell, Douglas M. *The Law in Classical Athens.* London: Thames and Hudson, 1978.

Mansfield, Harvey C., Jr. 'Aristotle: The Absent Executive in the Mixed Regime'. Chapter 3 in his *Taming the Prince: The Ambivalence of Modern Executive Power.* New York: The Free Press, 1989.

Mulgan, Richard. 'Aristotle's Analysis of Oligarchy and Democracy'. In *A Companion to Aristotle's* Politics. Ed. David Keyt and Fred D. Miller, Jr. Oxford: Blackwell, 1991. pp. 307–22.

Newell, W. R. 'Superlative Virtue: The Problem of Monarchy in Aristotle's "*Politics.*"' *Western Political Quarterly* 40, no. 1 (1987): 159–78.

Ober, Josiah. 'Aristotle's Natural Democracy'. In *Aristotle's* Politics: *Critical Essays.* Ed. Richard Kraut and Steven Skultety. Lanham, MD: Rowman & Littlefield, 2005. pp. 223–43.

Ostwald, Martin. *From Popular Sovereignty to the Sovereignty of Law: Law, Society, and Politics in Fifth-Century Athens.* Berkeley: University of California Press, 1986.

—. 'Was There a Concept *agraphos nomos* in Classical Greece? In *Exegesis and Argument: Studies in Greek Philosophy Presented to Gregory Vlastos.* Ed. E. N. Lee, A. P. D. Mourelatos, and R. M. Rorty. Assen: Van Gorcum, 1973. pp. 70–104.

Polin, Raymond. *Plato and Aristotle on Constitutionalism: An Exposition and Reference Source.* Brookfield, VT: Ashgate Publishing Company, 1998.

Swanson, Judith A. 'Aristotle on Public and Private Liberality and Justice'. In *Aristotelian Political Philosophy Volume I.* Ed. K. I. Boudouris.

Athens: International Center for Greek Philosophy and Culture & K.B., 1995. pp. 199–212.

—. 'Aristotle on How to Preserve a Regime: Maintaining Precedent, Privacy, and Peace through the Rule of Law'. In *Justice v. Law in Greek Political Thought*. Ed. Leslie G. Rubin. Lanham, MD: Rowman & Littlefield Publishers, Inc., 1997. pp. 153–82.

—. 'Aristotle on Liberality: Its Relation to Justice and Its Public and Private Practice'.*Polity: The Journal of the Northeastern Political Science Association* 27 (Fall 1994): 3–23.

Winthrop, Delba. 'Aristotle on Participatory Democracy'. *Polity* 11, no. 2 (1978): 151–71.

IX THE BEST REGIME

Bartlett, Robert C. 'The "Realism" of Classical Political Science: An Introduction to Aristotle's Best Regime'. In *Action and Contemplation: Studies in the Moral and Political Thought of Aristotle*. Ed. Robert C. Bartlett and Susan D. Collins. Albany, NY: State University of New York Press, 1999. pp. 293–313.

Huxley, George. 'On Aristotle's Best State'. *History of Political Thought* 6, no. 1/2 (1985): 139–49.

List, Charles J. 'The Virtues of Wild Leisure'. *Environmental Ethics* 27 (2005): 355–73.

Lord, Carnes. *Education and Culture in the Political Thought of Aristotle*. Ithaca: Cornell University Press, 1982.

Mara, Gerald M. 'The Role of Philosophy in Aristotle's Political Science'. *Polity* 19, no. 3 (1987): 375–401.

Solmsen, Friedrich. 'Leisure and Play in Aristotle's Ideal State'. *Rheinisches Museum fur Philogie* 107 (1964): 193–220.

Stocks, John Leofric. 'Schole'. *Classical Quarterly* 30 (1936): 177–87.

Vander Waerdt, P. A. 'Kingship and Philosophy in Aristotle's Best Regime'. *Phronesis* 30, no. 3 (1985): 249–73.

NOTES

I: CONTEXT

1 *The Complete Essays of Montaigne*, trans. Donald M. Frame. Stanford: Stanford University Press, 1958. p. 376.

2 Parmenides' claim of one pure Being, available to intuition, 'gives us the discovery of the intelligible world as an independent entity'. Snell, Bruno. *The Discovery of the Mind in Greek Philosophy and Literature.* New York: Dover Publications, Inc., 1982. p. 149.

3 'Speech harbours the seeds of the structure of the human intellect; the growth of human language, and finally the effort of philosophical thinking are necessary to allow that structure to unfold itself fully' (ibid., 245).

4 'Socrates breaks with the tradition which we have traced beginning with Homer, and, as Cicero puts it, restores philosophy from the sky to its place on the earth' (ibid., 151–2). See also Strauss, Leo. *The City and Man*, chapters I and II. Chicago: University of Chicago Press, 1964.

5 Thus Aristotle detects a problem inherent to the principle of democracy and was not an uncritical partisan of the Athenian regime in which he lived most of his life. The settling of differences of opinion quantitatively rather than qualitatively privileges will over reason. Democracy does not prevent the coincidence of will and reason, but because it makes the will of the majority politically authoritative whether or not it is reasonable, democracy encourages citizens to determine collectively what they want, rather than what they think is reasonable. Reasoned argument is at best and by chance only one among many means that citizens use to produce a majority consensus. In other words, because democracy guarantees that the will of the majority wins, it guarantees that reason never wins, except incidentally or secondarily by winning over will. Democracy is not simply neutral towards reason, but biased against it.

6 For a similar account see Swanson, Judith A. 'Aristotle on Nature, Human Nature, and Justice'. In *Action and Contemplation: Studies in the Moral and Political Thought of Aristotle*. Ed. Robert C. Bartlett and Susan D. Collins. Albany: State University of New York Press, 1999. pp. 240–2.

7 See especially *Nicomachean Ethics* V.7.

8 Hence a polity could never take the form of a world-state.

9 See also Ambler, Wayne H. 'Aristotle's Understanding of the Naturalness of the City', *The Review of Politics* 47, no. 2 (April 1985): 177.

10 As Eric Voegelin explains, 'What matters is not correct principles about what is right by nature in an immutable generality, nor [even]

the acute consciousness of the tension between the immutable truth and its mutable application . . . but the changeability, the *kineton* itself, and the methods to lift it to the reality of truth. . . . The *kineton* of action is the *locus* where man attains his truth. The truth of existence is attained where it becomes concrete, i.e., in action' ('What is Right by Nature?' in *Anamnesis*, trans. and ed. Gerhart Niemeyer. Notre Dame: University of Notre Dame Press, 1978. p. 63.

11 As Voegelin explains, the divine principle (*arche*) of the cosmos can use human instrumentalities of reason, knowledge and habits of virtue, or it can take a short cut directly to human action. 'The normal case is not that of the fortune-favored unwise, but rather that of the wise man. . . . Insofar as . . . [the wise man's] knowledge is the instrument used by the divine to attain truth in the reality of action, ethics itself is a phase in the movement of being that ends in the *kineton*, and its creation is a labor of serving the unmoved mover. The philosophical achievement of ethics has its dignity as a part of the divine movement that leads to the truth of action' (ibid., p. 64).

12 This section appears in Swanson, 'Aristotle on Nature, Human Nature, and Justice'. pp. 226–9.

13 Aristotle, *Metaphysics*, trans. Hugh Tredennick. Cambridge: Harvard University Press, 1935. See also Pierre Pellegrin, 'Logical Difference and Biological Difference: The Unity of Aristotle's Thought'. In *Philosophical Issues in Aristotle's Biology*. Ed. Allan Gotthelf and James G. Lennox. Cambridge: Cambridge University Press, 1987. pp. 321–2.

14 See also Pellegrin, 'Logical Difference'. pp. 321–2.

15 Ibid., pp. 330.

II: OVERVIEW OF THEMES

1 Carnes Lord, 'The Character and Composition of Aristotle's *Politics*', *Political Theory* 9, no. 4 (1981): 45–60.

2 'La "Politique" d'Aristote: Unité et fractures éloge de la lecture sommaire', *Revue Philosophique de la France et de L'étranger* 177, no. 2 (1987): 133.

3 'Character and Composition', pp. 459, 469.

4 Ibid., p. 460. The view also of Lord, 'Character and Composition', pp. 470–1.

5 Jaeger, *Aristotle: Fundamentals of the History of His Development*. 2nd edn. Trans. Richard Robinson. Oxford: Clarendon, 1948. pp. 263–75.

6 Furthermore, Aristotle's discussion of the good household in Books I and II serves to explain his claim in the *Nicomachean Ethics* that individuals may cultivate moral virtue independently of the regime in which they live. As P. A. Vander Waerdt remarks, 'there is no suggestion in *EN* x 9 that a father who lives in an inferior regime should educate his children in accordance with its inferior ends'.

'The Political Intention of Aristotle's Moral Philosophy', *Ancient Philosophy* 5, no. 1 (1985): 87.
7 Jaeger, *Aristotle*, pp. 267, 273.
8 'Political Intention', pp. 87–8.
9 Jaffa goes on to explain that 'in Book I, the understanding of the generation of the *polis* implied an understanding of its perfection – i.e., the best regime – because to understand the generation of anything that exists by nature means to understand the activity of that thing when it has attained its perfection. . . . Book II examined a number of regimes . . . and they were found wanting. But the principle in virtue of which Aristotle noted those deficiencies was the principle of the best regime. Book III culminated in the examination of the principal rival claims to supreme power in the *polis*. . . . The reconciliation of these claims . . . itself constituted the principle of the best regime. Books IV, V and VI demonstrate the different manners in which this reconciliation or harmonization takes place when external conditions forbid its full implementation'. 'Aristotle'. In *History of Political Philosophy*. 2nd edn. Ed. Leo Strauss and Joseph Cropsey. Chicago: University of Chicago Press, 1972. pp. 125–6.
10 See also Pellegrin, 'La "Politique" d'Aristote'. pp.137–58.
11 The above discussion is an adaptation of Judith A. Swanson, *The Public and the Private in Aristotle's Political Philosophy*. Ithaca: Cornell University Press, 1992. pp. 222–5.
12 For a fuller account see Swanson, *The Public and the Private in Aristotle's Political Philosophy*.

IV: RECEPTION AND INFLUENCE

1 See Carter, L. B. *The Quiet Athenian*. Oxford: Clarendon, 1986.
2 Sabine, George Holland and Smith, Stanley Barney, 'Introduction'. In Cicero, Marcus Tullius. *On the Commonwealth*. Indianapolis: Bobbs-Merrill Educational Publishing, 1976. pp. 39–40.
3 P. G. Walsh observes that 'The Peripatetics, whose influence following the deaths of Aristotle and his successor Theophrastus had declined for almost two centuries, gained new strength in the first century B.C. under Andronicus of Rhodes; Aristotle's writings emerged at that time from obscurity, and the *Nicomachean Ethics* stimulated discussion about the Chief Good among the rival schools'. 'Introduction to Cicero'. *On Obligations*, trans. P. G. Walsh. Oxford University Press, 2000. p. xxxi.
4 Ibid., 1. 2.
5 *Orator*, trans. H. M. Hubbell. Cambridge: Harvard University Press, 1988. p. 5.
6 Ibid., pp. 46, 114, 172, 192, 194, 214, 218, 228.
7 Ibid., pp. 62–4. I have slightly modified the phrase order.

8 *On the Commonwealth*. p. 106.
9 *On the Commonwealth*. 'Introduction'. pp. 95, 215. Because this work is a dialogue and the interlocutor Laelius makes this claim, there cannot be certainty that it expresses Cicero's own view, but logic of the arguments indicates that the remark constitutes a prevailing, and thus possibly Ciceronian, view.
10 Ibid., p. 216.
11 Ibid., pp. 38, 99. According to Sabine and Smith, then, 'we may fairly claim Cicero's conception of the state marks the intermediate stage between the city-state of which Aristotle made so profound an analysis and the world-state of which the Edict of Caracalla is the symbol and expression'.
12 Ibid., p. 231 n31.
13 *On Obligations*, 3.35; see also Sabine and Smith. ' Introduction'. *On the Commonwealth*. pp. 98–9.
14 *On the Commonwealth*, III. Sabine and Smith note that 'a belief in the higher ethical function of the state, as opposed to a merely utilitarian view, was an important issue between the Stoics and the Epicureans' (p. 231 n11).
15 St Augustine, *Concerning the City of God against the Pagans*. Trans. Henry Bettensen. London: Penguin Books, 1984. pp. 315–16.
16 *Alfarabi, The Political Writings: Selected Aphorisms and Other Texts*. Trans. Charles E. Butterworth. Ithaca: Cornell University Press, 2001. pp. ix, xi–xii, 7, 9, 164–8.
17 Ibid., Aphorism #74, p. 164.
18 Ibid., pp. 119–27, 150–4.
19 Ibid., pp. 129–45, 153–7, 162, 165–7 (Aphorisms #77–9).
20 Averroes, 'The Decisive Treatise, Determining What the Connection is Between Religion and Philosophy'. In *Medieval Political Philosophy*. p. 173; *The Cambridge Dictionary of Philosophy*. 2nd edn. Ed. Robert Audi. Cambridge: Cambridge University Press, 1999. p. 63.
21 'The Decisive Treatise'. pp. 173–4.
22 'Guide of the Perplexed'. In *Medieval Political Philosophy*. Ed. Ralph Lerner and Muhsin Mahdi. Ithaca: Cornell University Press, 1972. pp. 196–7.
23 Ibid., pp. 203–04.
24 Maimonides, 'Logic', chapter XIV [Political Science] in *Medieval Political Philosophy*. pp. 189–90.
25 *Summa Theologica*, I–II, Question 94, Fourth and Fifth Articles; II–II, Question 11, Third Article. St Thomas permits the church to excommunicate heretics and turn their fate over to the judgement of secular courts.
26 Dante, 'On Monarchy'. Trans. Philip H. Wicksteed. In *Medieval Political Philosophy*. pp. 418–38.
27 *Defensor Pacis*, I.4.1, 4; I.6.9. For a more comprehensive commentary that informs this one, see Strauss, Leo. 'Marsilius of Padua'. In *History of Political Philosophy*. 3rd. edn. Ed. Leo Strauss and Joseph Cropsey. Chicago: University of Chicago Press, 1987. pp. 276–95.

28 Luther, Martin. 'Address to the German Nobility'. In *The Prince, Utopia, Ninety-Five Theses*. New York: The Collier Press, 1910. p. 338.
29 William J. Bouwsma, *John Calvin: A Sixteenth-Century Portrait*. New York: Oxford University Press, 1988. pp. 99, 114.
30 Serm. No. 103 on Job, 522–3; cf. *Institutes*, II, ii, 16.
31 Serm. No. 36 on Deut., 313; Comm. Is. 2:3.
32 Comm. Ezek. 9:3–4.
33 Bouwsma, op. cit., pp. 14, 164; Comms. Gen. 19:24, Ps. 107:43.
34 *The Philosophy of Francis Bacon*. Ed. Benjamin Farrington. Liverpool: Liverpool University Press, 1964. pp. 19, 42, 83, 112.
35 Ibid., p. 115.
36 Ibid., p. 112.
37 See Jean-Jacques Rousseau, *On the Social Contract* and *Second Discourse*.
38 Smith, Adam. *The Theory of Moral Sentiments*. Indianapolis: Liberty Classics, 1982. pp. 196n., 210, 269–73.
39 Madison, James. 'Report of Books'. In *The Papers of James Madison*. Ed. Robert A. Rutland et al. Chicago: University of Chicago Press, 1962–1977. vol. 6, pp. 76–7.
40 Miller Jr., Fred D. 'Aristotle and American Classical Republicanism'. In *Justice v. Law in Greek Political Thought*. Ed. Leslie G. Rubin. Lanham, MD: Rowman & Littlefield Publishers, Inc., 1997. p. 184.
41 Ibid., pp. 184–8.
42 At the beginning of Federalist #9, Hamilton notes: 'It is impossible to read the history of the petty republics of Greece and Italy without feeling sensations of horror and disgust at the distractions with which they were continually agitated and at the succession of revolutions by which they were kept in a state of perpetual vibration between the extremes of tyranny and anarchy.'
43 Federalist #10.
44 Richard, Carl J. *The Founders and the Classics: Greece, Rome, and the American Enlightenment*. Cambridge: Harvard University Press, 1994. p. 230.
45 See, for example, ibid., p. 97 and Miller, 'Aristotle and American Classical Republicanism'. p. 191.
46 Richard, *Founders and the Classics*. p. 230.
47 Alexis de Tocqueville, *Democracy in America*. Trans. and ed., Harvey C. Mansfield and Delba Winthrop. Chicago: University of Chicago Press, 2000. p. 413.
48 Ibid., pp. 251–8.
49 Ibid., pp. 451–2.
50 Mill, John Stuart. *On Liberty*. Ed. Gertrude Himmelfarb. New York: Penguin Books, 1982. p. 63.
51 Accordingly, Shirley Robin Letwin notes that '*On Liberty* was not a defence of the common man's right to live as he liked; it was more nearly an attack on him'. *The Pursuit of Certainty*. Cambridge:

Cambridge University Press, 1965. p. 301. See also Himmelfarb, Gertrude. *On Liberty and Liberalism: The Case of John Stuart Mill.* San Francisco: Institute for Contemporary Studies, 1990.

52 Marx, Karl. 'Economic and Philosophic Manuscripts of 1844: Selections', p. 78; 'Capital: Selections', pp. 229n–230n, 294; Engels, Friedrich. 'Socialism: Utopian and Scientific'. p. 616 in *The Marx-Engels Reader*. Ed. Robert C. Tucker. New York: W. W. Norton & Company, Inc. 1972.

53 See Strauss, Leo. 'On Aristotle's Politics'. In *The City and Man.* Chicago: The University of Chicago Press, 1964 and *Natural Right and History.* Chicago: University of Chicago Press, 1957; Arendt, Hannah. *The Human Condition.* Chicago: University of Chicago Press, 1958. chapters I and II; Oakeshott, Michael. *On Human Conduct.* Oxford: Clarendon Press, 1975. pp 109–11; and Rawls, John. *A Theory of Justice.* Cambridge: Harvard University Press, 1971. pp. 92, 424–33.

54 See. Nussbaum, Martha C and Sen, Amartya. *The Quality of Life.* Oxford: Oxford University Press, 1993; MacIntyre, Alasdair. *After Virtue: A Study in Moral Theory.* Notre Dame: University of Notre Dame Press, 1981 and *Whose Justice? Which Rationality?* Notre Dame: University of Notre Dame Press, 1988.

INDEX

abortion 119
accountability 51–2
acquisition 23
  modes of 28–33, 146
  of possessions 108–9
Adams, John 142
Aeschylus 3
affluence 70, 71, 72, 74, 75, 87,
  88, 89, 90, 92, 94, 104
agriculture 29, 31–2, 33, 102, 114
  see also farming
Alcibiades 87
Alexander the Great 1, 113
Alfarabi 131–3
ambition 41, 109–10, 117
Amyntas (King) 1
Andronicus of Rhodes 157n3
animals 25, 29, 31, 135
  compared with cities 70–1
  psychological traits of 7, 19
Antisthenes 62
Apollonia 70
appetite(s) 12, 119, 134
  see also desires
Aquinas, Saint Thomas 135–6
Archidamus 90
Arendt, Hannah 147
aristocracy 40, 47, 54, 64–5, 67,
  75–6, 79, 84, 90
aristocrats 83–4
Aristotle: biographical and
    intellectual
    background 1–3
  context of writings of 1–8
  philosophic perspective of 2

Aristotelian corpus, unity of
  5–8
armed forces *see* military power
artisans 31, 39, 42, 53
Asians 113
Athens 1–2, 4, 11, 45, 49, 50, 85,
  86, 87, 89, 90, 128, 155n5,
  159n42
Athens Academy 1, 131
athletic training 66–8, 71
Augustine, Saint 130–1
authority: of law 72
  political 58–65
Averroes 133

Bacon, Francis 139–40
Baghdad 132
beauty 27, 92
bioethics 7
biology 7
bodily goods 109–10
body 6–7, 25, 123
business expertise 30–3

Calvin, John 137–9
capital punishment 136
capitalism 146–7
Carthage 35, 43–5, 49
categories 5–6, 7–8
cavalry 44, 104
chance 31, 45, 102, 116
change 42–3
character 7, 122, 126, 146
  goodness of 62
Charondas 46

children 23, 34
  care of 119–20
  communal ownership of 37–8
  education of 121–7, 156n6
  rule over 33–4, 53–4
choice-making 5, 18, 21, 57, 116
choice-worthy life 108–10, 117
Christianity 135–6, 137, 139
Church 137, 158n25
Cicero, Marcus Tullius 128–30,
  155n4, 158n9, 158n11
citizens: associations among 95,
  103, 115–16
  character of 113
  definition of 48–9, 50, 54
  in democracy 49, 72, 75, 102–3,
  155n5
  education of 93, 116–17
  virtue of 10, 52–3, 75, 113–14
citizenship 48–9
  origin of 49–51
city 6
  compared with animal 70–1
  definition of 47–8, 49
  division of 13, 115
  household and 19
  ideal size 112–13
  identity of 51–4
  interdependence of 37
  naturalness of 10, 11, 12–13,
  16–22, 128
  origin of 17–19
  paradoxical character of 12,
  15, 22
  purpose of 16–17, 57
  unity of 16, 37
The City of God
  (Augustine) 130–1
civic organizations 103
classes 5–6, 7–8
Cleisthenes 50
clergy 136–7
  see also priesthood

collective judgement 59–60,
  155n5
Colophonia 70
commerce 29–30
communism 37–8, 39
conflict 19, 21–2, 44, 87, 146
  factional 39, 77, 82–5, 87
consent 21
Constitution, U. S. 103, 118,
  141–3
constitutional transformation 84
  see also regimes: change
  revolution
contraries 8
convention 4, 6, 10, 12–13, 17,
  20, 62, 131
corruption 44, 73, 74–5, 83, 91,
  94, 110
courage 30, 32, 34, 94, 111, 118,
  119, 122, 123, 124
courts 45, 60, 79, 158n25
Crete 35, 43–5
crime 37, 39, 41, 46, 49
culture 86, 122, 128
  see also character
  tribal identity
customs 64

Dante Alighieri 136
deceit 85–6, 87
decision-making offices 49, 50,
  78–9, 102
demagogues 88, 89
democracy 47, 54, 55–61,
  67–75, 79, 84, 96, 100,
  155n5
  citizens in 49, 72, 75, 102–3,
  155n5
  direct 88–9
  factional conflict in 84–5
  freedom and 100–2
  regime change and 88–90
  tyrannical 73, 159n42

Democracy in America
   (Tocqueville) 143–5
democratization 44, 45
depravity 25, 39, 86
desert 44, 47, 61, 62, 94
  see also merit
desires 6, 16–17, 20, 30–1, 38, 41,
   86, 109–10
dictators 63, 77
dispositions 38, 66, 80
divine 3, 5, 8, 18, 19, 131–3, 135,
   136, 137, 156n11
divine control 21
divine right 130, 137, 139
dogmatism 2
Douglas, Stephen 101
dowries 44
Draco 46
duality, of nature 8
dynasty 44, 73, 75, 78

economy 18, 28–33, 118, 141, 146
Edict of Caracalla 158n11
education 34, 39, 41, 113
  of children 34, 121–7
  democratic 93
  oligarchic 93
  physical 123
  political 108, 117–19, 122
Egyptian regime 70
election laws 60, 78, 85–6
election reform 88–9
Enlightenment thought 13
Epicureans 158n14
equality 72, 73, 83, 84, 91
eros 41
eternalism 132–3
ethics 4–5, 7, 156n11, 158n14
Europeans, Northern 113
excellence 34, 47, 53, 116–17, 122,
   146
exercise 123
extremism 82, 93, 159n42

factional conflict 82–8
family 18, 19, 57
  see also lineage
farming 29, 31–2, 33, 44, 74, 102,
   114
  see also agriculture
fathers 23, 33, 37, 156n6
Federalist Papers 142, 143, 159n42
females *see* sexes; women
force 25, 27, 87, 89, 114
foreign policy 39, 44, 77, 103–4,
   113
foreigners 29, 44, 48, 50, 54, 55,
   115
form 6–7
Founding Fathers 141–3
free market 115–16
  see also commerce
free speech 12
freedom 47, 58, 66, 70, 73, 99,
   100–5, 112–13

generosity 38
  of nature 17
God 129, 130, 131–4, 136–8
Gods 18, 21, 128
goods: bodily 109–10
  external 108–10
  see also material goods
governments: accountability
  of 51–2
Greeks 2, 113, 128
Grotius 143
Guide of the Perplexed
  (Maimonides) 134–5

Hamilton, Alexander 142, 159n42
happiness 2, 10, 25, 39, 107–12,
   114, 116, 118, 146
  see also pleasure seeking
harmony 5, 35, 39, 122
Hegel (G. W. F) 97, 147
Hellenism 128

Heraclitus 3
herdsmen 102–3
  see also nomadism
heretics 158n25
Herpyllis 2
Hesiod 18
Hippodamus 35, 36, 42–3
History of Animals (Aristotle) 7
Hobbes, Thomas 139–40
Homer 3, 155n4
household 15–16, 18, 19, 39
  acquisition by 28–33
  moral significance of 10, 156n6
household management 22–3,
    31, 34
human constraints 21
human nature 12, 20–1, 22, 146–7
human soul *see* soul
husbands 23, 33–4

ideal regime 108
ideology 77, 80, 93, 143
imperialism 45
incest 37
inequality 83, 84, 102
inheritance 44, 87
injustice 58, 59
intellect 3, 119, 132, 155n3
intellectual virtue 34
intuition (*nous*) 4
Islamic political
    philosophy 131–3

Jaeger, Werner 9, 10
Jaffa, Harry V. 11, 157n9
Jason 53
Jay, John 142
Jefferson, Thomas 143
Jesus Christ 131
Jewish philosophy 131, 133–5
judgement 20–1, 57
  collective 59–60, 62
  political 61, 70, 71, 72, 78–9,
    114

judges 79, 105
jury duty 45, 82, 144–5
just rule 62
justice 20, 47, 56, 61, 71, 100
justice, natural 4–5
    see also natural right
justice, political 4, 61–3

kings 18
kingship 47, 54, 59, 63–5, 67,
    94–6, 129
    see also monarchy
knowledge: objective 3
  practice and 15
Koran 133

land, ownership of 38
law-abidingness 56
lawlessness 77, 91, 93
law(s) 20
  authority of 72
  changing 42–3
  crafting 45
  in democracy 71–2
  natural 130, 136
  physical 4
  quality of 60–1
  rule of 58–9, 64, 89
  unjust 61
The Laws (Plato) 35–6, 39–40
leadership 33, 40, 62–3, 88, 92,
    116, 117
leisure 13, 43, 44, 45, 74, 103,
    119, 121–3
Leviathan (Hobbes) 140
liberality 72, 94
(*On*) *Liberty* (Mill) 145–6
licentiousness 21–2, 44, 95, 103
Lincoln, Abraham 101
lineage 62
living well 2, 20, 57
Lord, Carnes vii, 9, 156n1, 156n4
love affairs 86–7
lumbering 31, 32

Luther, Martin 137–8
Lyceum 1
Lycurgus 45

MacIntyre, Alasdair 147–8
Madison, James 141, 142
Maimonides 131, 133–5
majority rule 58, 101, 155n5
  see also collective judgement
    democracy
male-female relationships 18, 23,
  33–4
man, as political animal 11–12,
  19–20
manliness 110, 115, 128
markets: common 115–16
  free 115–16
marriage 33, 57
Marsilius of Padua 136–7
Marx, Karl 97, 146–7
masters 17, 23, 24
master-slave relationship 24–8
mastery 23, 34, 53, 110, 114
material goods 28–9, 41
  see also goods: external
matter 6–7
merit 61
  see also desert
merits, rewards based on 91,
  114–15
Metaphysics (Aristotle) 7
middle class 74–5, 76
military leadership 26–7, 63, 65,
  92, 105, 114
military power 45, 61, 70, 104
military regimes 88, 110
Mill, John Stuart 143, 145–6
mind 3, 31, 131, 146
mining 31, 32
mixed regimes 39–40, 73–4, 76,
  78, 79, 143
moderation
  political 76–7, 82–3, 93, 103
  virtue of 34, 53, 118

monarchy 40, 76–7, 94–6
  see also kingship; tyranny
money 29–31
money-making 15, 29–33
monogamy 38
monopoly 32
monotheism 131
Montaigne 2
moral and intellectual virtue 34,
  122
moral virtue 10, 134–6, 156n6
mothers 23, 34, 37
music 121–2, 123–7

natural justice, Aristotle's
  concept of 4–5
natural law 130, 136
natural plurality 6–8
natural right 4, 136, 147, 155–6n10
natural slaves 26–8
nature 4–6, 12
  city and 10, 11, 16–22
  constraints of 21
  human nature 20–1, 22
nepotism 73
  see also dynasty
Nicomachean Ethics
  (Aristotle) 6, 8, 25, 41, 47,
  56, 58, 134, 156n6, 155n7,
  157n3
Nicomachus 1
nomadism 29
non-Western philosophers
  131–5
Nussbaum, Martha C. 147

Oakeshott, Michael 147
objectivity 3
(*On*) *Obligations* (Cicero) 129–30
observation 16–17, 22
office-holders 114–15
  attributes of 92–3
  criteria for 59–60, 72, 73
  selection of 78–9

offices 48, 49, 78, 105
oligarchy 39–40, 44–5, 47, 54,
    55–8, 67–75, 78, 79, 84,
    96, 100
  effective rule within 91–2
  factional conflict in 84–5
  orderliness and 104–5
  revolution within 89–90
Olympic Gods 3, 13, 117
opinion 155n5
orderliness 99, 100, 104–5,
    112–13
ostracism 63
outstanding individuals 62–3

papal power 136–7
parental rule 23
parent-child relationships 33–4
Parmenides 3, 155n2
partisanship 77, 78, 79–80, 83, 86
partnerships 16, 17–18
parts: of city 15–21, 68
  of households 23
  of regime 11
  rule and 24–5
paternal rule 23
peace 57, 78, 113, 118–19
Pellegrin, Pierre 9, 156n13–15,
    157n10
Peloponnesian War 89, 90
Periander 63, 94
Pericles 45, 90
Peripatetic pedagogy 1, 131, 157n3
Persians 45
Phaleas 35, 40–2, 46
Philip II (King) 1
Philolaus 46
philosopher-king 70, 96
philosophy 8, 13, 22, 28, 41, 66,
    109, 112, 118, 122, 136,
    155n3, 156n11
  criticism of 129
  education and 119, 121–2, 126
  Islamic 131–3

Jewish 131, 133–5
  political 2, 3, 22, 36, 55, 128,
    129–33
physical education 123
physical laws 4
Pittacus 46
Plato 1–3, 13, 36, 41, 46, 68, 83,
    96–8, 130, 131, 132, 133,
    147
  see also The Republic; Socrates
pleasure 38, 41, 122
pleasure seeking 41, 94, 146
plurality 7, 8
poetry 29, 59
political authority 58–65
political diversification 103
political education 108, 117–19
political expertise (vs mastery) 110
  see also judgement
political institutions 78
political justice 4, 61–3
political life 13
political moderation see
    moderation
political nature 11–12, 19–20
political participation 50, 52, 101
  in democracy 72
  see also citizens
political partnership 16
political problems, solutions to 80
political science 1, 3, 6, 10, 61,
    66–7, 71, 80, 83, 98
political unity 35
politics 21, 22, 28, 116, 122, 136
  origin of 12
Politics (Aristotle): context
    of 2–8
  order of books in 9–10, 11
  overview of themes in 9–14
polity 47, 54, 64–5, 67–8, 75–7,
    79, 84, 90
poor 71–2
  rule by 57–8
  support of 103–4

popular leaders, ancient 88
popular rule 100–1
population size 112–13
poverty 32, 39, 55, 57–8, 61
power, acquisition of 91
praise *see* recognition, desire for
prayer 11, 13, 21, 35, 116
pre-Socratic philosophers 3
priesthood 13, 115, 136
private disputes 86–7, 89
private ownership 38, 39
private sphere 13
progress 43
property: communal ownership
    of 37–8
  distribution of 40–2
  division of 115
  private ownership of 38, 39
prudence 53–4
public sphere 13
Pythagoras 3
Pythias 2

quality 55, 70, 71, 77–8, 84, 85,
    112, 155n5
quantity 55, 70, 71, 77–8, 84, 85,
    102, 112, 155n5
Quietist movement 128

Rawls, John 147
reason 3, 15, 16, 26, 57, 70,
    155n5, 156n11
  see also intellect; philosophy
recognition, desire for 41, 59–60,
    77, 94, 110
redistribution, of wealth 40–2,
    58, 82, 88, 103–4
regicide 94
regimes: best 10–11, 35–40, 66–8,
    79, 107, 113–14, 157n9
  best possible 66, 68, 77, 79,
    112
  change 73–4, 83–90, 96–8
  crafting 45

existing 43–6
ideal 108
maintenance of 83–5, 91–6
mixed 73–4, 76, 78, 79
naturalness of 12
nature of best 11–12
Socrates' view of best 36–40
types of 13–14, 47, 54–5
variation 68–9
variety within 100
religious institutions 104, 114,
    115
  see also priesthood
representation, political 88
reproduction 17, 19
The Republic (Plato) 35–6, 38,
    39, 40, 62, 70, 83, 96–8,
    100
revolution 82–90, 94, 96–8, 146
rhetoric 88
rights 136, 144, 147
Rome 128, 144
Rousseau, Jean-Jacques 140–1
rule by law 58–9, 64, 89
rulers 49
  attributes of 53–4, 92–3
  oligarchic 91–2
rules, accountability of 51–2
ruling 10, 15, 24–5

schools 39
self-preservation 17, 38
self-sufficiency 6, 11, 19, 22, 29, 49
Sen, Amartya 147
serfs 43–4
servility 53–4
sexes: household roles of 33–4
  relationships between 18, 23,
    33–4
sight (political discernment) 72, 86
slavery 24–8
slaves 23, 24, 48, 53–4
  natural 17, 26–8
  procurement of 28, 29

Smith, Adam 141
social class 47, 114
social contract 13, 21
social functions 114–15
society 48
Socrates 3, 35–40, 70, 83, 96–8,
    100, 113, 155n4
Solon 29, 45
Sophocles 3
soul 6–7, 25, 38, 108, 117,
    132
Sparta 35, 38, 43–5, 49, 76, 90,
    110, 118, 119
speech 15, 19, 22, 26, 155n3
spiritedness 96, 113, 114
Stagira 1
Stoics 158n14
Strauss, Leo 147, 155n4,
    158n27

teleology 6, 10, 16–17, 146
temperance 41, 134
    see also moderation
territorial differences 86
Thales of Miletus 32
Theophrastus 157n3
Theopompus 96
Therea 70
Thrasyboulus 63, 94
timocracy 96, 97
Tocqueville, Alexis de 143–5
toleration 103
tribal identity 18, 86, 88
truth(s) 3, 13, 155–6n10
tyranny 13, 47, 54, 63, 67–8, 73,
    75, 76–7, 83, 88, 94–6, 97,
    100, 102, 159n42

unity 7, 8
    of city 16, 37
    political 35
unjust laws 61
urban democracies 103

U. S. Constitution 103, 118, 141–3
(On) Utilitarianism (Mill) 145–6

Vander Waerdt, P. A. 10–11,
    156–7n6
villages 18–19
virtue 10, 34, 47, 56, 62, 107,
    110–11, 113–14, 116
    of citizens 10, 52–3, 75, 113–14
    intellectual 34, 156n11
    justice and 63
    moral 10, 134–6, 156n6
    moral and intellectual 34, 122
    of the multitude 54–5
    political 71
virtuous 84, 108–12, 114
Voegelin, Eric 155–6n10, 156n11

war 29, 44, 78, 88, 95, 111, 118,
    119, 128
wealth 47, 62
    acquisition of 28–33
    disparity in 69
    merits of 66
    possession of 109
    redistribution of 40–2, 58, 88,
        103–4
    see also affluence
wealthy 71–2
    rule by 57–8, 75
William of Moerbeke 135
Wilson, James 143
wisdom 5, 29, 134
wives 23, 33–4, 54
women 17–18
    communal ownership of 37–8
    relationships between men
        and 33–4, 53
    Spartan 44
    value of 57
    see also sexes

Zeno 130